Anna Romandash

Women of Ukraine

Reportages from the War and Beyond,
2022 - 2023

UKRAINIAN VOICES

Collected by Andreas Umland

The book series "Ukrainian Voices" publishes English- and German-language monographs, edited volumes, document collections, and anthologies of articles authored and composed by Ukrainian politicians, intellectuals, activists, officials, researchers, and diplomats. The series' aim is to introduce Western and other audiences to Ukrainian explorations, deliberations and interpretations of historic and current, domestic, and international affairs. The purpose of these books is to make non-Ukrainian readers familiar with how some prominent Ukrainians approach, view and assess their country's development and position in the world. The series was founded, and the volumes are collected by Andreas Umland, Dr. phil. (FU Berlin), Ph. D. (Cambridge), Associate Professor of Politics at the Kyiv-Mohyla Academy and an Analyst in the Stockholm Centre for Eastern European Studies at the Swedish Institute of International Affairs.

Anna Romandash

WOMEN OF UKRAINE

Reportages from the War and Beyond,
2022 - 2023

Bibliographic information published by the Deutsche Nationalbibliothek

Die Deutsche Nationalbibliothek lists this publication in the Deutsche Nationalbibliografie; detailed bibliographic data are available in the Internet at http://dnb.d-nb.de.

Bibliografische Information der Deutschen Nationalbibliothek

Die Deutsche Nationalbibliothek verzeichnet diese Publikation in der Deutschen Nationalbibliografie; detaillierte bibliografische Daten sind im Internet über http://dnb.d-nb.de abrufbar.

Cover pictures: Unsplash / Farrinni,
Unsplash / Oksana Manych,
ID 91321459 © Anton Unguryanu | Dreamstime.com,
ID 158189507 © Ivan Kuzkin | Dreamstime.com,
ID 243801217 © Oleksandr Lypa | Dreamstime.com

ISBN-13: 978-3-8382-1819-9

© *ibidem*-Verlag, Stuttgart 2023

Printed in the United States of America

Contents

Awakening to Russian Aggression

The Invasion of Ukraine Must Stir the Global Community to Action in Support of a Besieged Nation and the Human Rights at Stake in the Fight

February/March 2022

I could not sleep on the night of February 24. Something was amiss. I grabbed my phone and checked the news. Then I knew it. Russia had invaded Ukraine—something we all feared but did not want to believe would happen. I called my mom right away.

"What a bastard," she said, bitterness and anger in her voice.

She was referring to Vladimir Putin, the President of Russia, who, hours earlier, announced a "special military operation" into Ukraine. The operation turned out to be a full-scale war, targeting major cities in Ukraine and killing hundreds of civilians to date, with nearly a million refugees fleeing the country. Yet the fight continues.

I am a journalist by training, but I am not going to pretend I am an impartial observer. And who can be when a sovereign country is invaded by a much larger neighbor, a bully with nukes and a giant army that is willing to follow any order—even when that means killing innocent people.

I am grateful to people around the world supporting Ukraine. This is not a question of politics; it is a matter of humanity, of helping fellow humans in need who are being senselessly murdered and whose homes are being destroyed.

As you may know, the Kremlin is trying to shift the war blame onto Ukrainians. They refuse to admit Russian military losses and deny the murders of Ukrainian civilians.

For the world, it is important to understand that the most recent lies are only the latest words of a propaganda machine launched by the Kremlin against Ukraine during the last decade, and that propaganda has been transmitted in the West thanks to media polarization across many countries.

For instance, in 2014, Russia annexed the Southern Ukrainian peninsula of Crimea; in addition, the Kremlin initiated and supported separatism in Eastern Ukraine, where it created two puppet regimes aimed at destabilizing the rest of the country. Some Western sanctions were imposed as a result, but they were not strong enough to affect the Russian government. The Kremlin quickly adapted and continued with its sadly successful Ukraine-phobic propaganda.

For many years, Western leaders tried to maintain the notion that everything was fine. Russia was still invited to international conferences, and the Kremlin remained an important global political voice. Despite other ways to meet its energy needs, Europe's dependence on Russian gas has blinded the continent to the Kremlin using its natural resource as leverage.

Now even the biggest Putin defenders realize the danger of the Russian regime. Sanctions that harm the oligarchs have been imposed, but bullets still target the Ukrainian people. Russian missiles bomb cities and villages from unprotected skies. NATO and its major members — such as the United States and Great Britain — refuse to interfere. Ukrainian fighters remain largely on their own, defending their country as Russia wages full-scale war with one of the biggest armies in the world.

And the Kremlin is treating its troops as artillery meat. If Russian soldiers get killed, the government will just send new ones. Therefore, greater intervention is needed. Everyone who supports Ukraine can help to facilitate that — spreading the word about what's happening, mobilizing communities, contacting congressional representatives, and monitoring businesses.

There are still lots of American and European companies operating in Russia. They must leave immediately. The European Union is still buying Russian energy and sending millions in revenue back to Russia. This needs to change. The Russian economy — just like its leader — needs to be isolated from the world over this aggression.

Ukraine also needs military help to arm its forces to fight the Russian army. In my home region of Lviv, the number of volunteers far exceeds the arms available. Donations to trusted organizations and advocacy for more support from governments around the world would help strengthen Ukraine.

This war is not only about Ukraine. It is about humanity and values, about the right to be free, to live in peace, and to protect your nation and your land.

I remember the cold winter of 2014 when millions of Ukrainians ousted corrupt President Viktor Yanukovych from power despite government violence against protesters on the streets of the capital, Kyiv. The Ukrainian people have even more resolve now.

They have nothing to lose but their country and their freedom.

Ukrainian Refugees:
The Decision to Go into the Unknown

The Exodus of Ukrainians Is the Biggest Refugee Crisis Europe Has Faced since the Second World War

March 2022

More than 1.5 million Ukrainians have fled the country in less than two weeks, and there are many more internally displaced people. However, the exact amount is much harder to measure. Western Ukrainian cities — which have received the greatest influx of internally displaced people — are almost at capacity.

The exodus of Ukrainians is the biggest refugee crisis Europe has faced since the Second World War, and it comes as a direct result of the Russian war on Ukraine. On February 24, 150,000 Russian soldiers started their invasion into the country. Nearly two weeks later, they destroyed various cities in the north and east of Ukraine and created a catastrophe in the cities under siege.

The refugees who crossed the Ukrainian border for neighboring countries mostly consist of women and children, but there are also a number of elderly and foreigners. All men aged 18 to 60 are required to remain in Ukraine in case they need to fight the Russian army.

The busiest border is between Ukraine and Poland, with the latter already having received more than one million refugees. On the other side of the border, people are met with volunteers ready to provide them with warm food, clothes and transport (they offer rides to different cities in Poland and beyond). Europeans have shown a very high level of solidarity with Ukrainians, opening their homes for free to people in search of a place to sleep and helping them find jobs.

Svitlana Lavochkina is a Ukrainian writer living in Leipzig with her German husband. She recently hosted Taya and Yana, both teenagers from Kyiv.

"On Monday, they will start school, which is free for them," Svitlana says, "They really want to study. Their mothers are happy too because there won't be any issues with their documents."

Taya, 15, and Yana, 17, arrived in Germany by themselves; their parents stayed in Ukraine to volunteer. Svitlana says she agreed to host them without even asking for their last names — she just wanted to help youth in need.

"More children will come," she concludes, "Leipzig will learn how Ukrainian kids can study despite everything."

Crossing the Border with Children

Many children don't understand what is happening to them as they depart from their homeland. Iryna Vyrtosu shares her story of crossing the Slovak border with her tiny daughter.

"I did not feel safe at home, even though I am from Western Ukraine," Vyrtosu explains, "I made a decision to leave in a flash."

Western Ukraine remains relatively safe. However, Russian troops have recently bombed the city of Vinnytsia, where they destroyed an airport and killed civilians during shelling.

As Iryna and her family departed for the border, they picked up two women trying to reach their homes further west in Ukraine. Those women later hosted Iryna's family before they fled the country.

"You meet many volunteers on your way," Iryna recalls, "They suggest the best routes to you and tell you which border crossing to choose."

Iryna's husband helped his wife and their daughter, Vlada, to get to the pedestrian border crossing to Slovakia.

"The line of refugees was growing, but it still moved forward, and that instilled some optimism in us," Iryna says, "On the tables by the line, sandwiches were served. There were pancakes with jam, as well as apples, cookies, yogurt, and hot tea. Food was abundant."

Iryna's husband stayed in Ukraine; he, like all drafted men, is not allowed to leave Ukraine.

"I don't know when I will see him again," Iryna said.

When mother and daughter reached Slovakia, the family, again, was greeted by many volunteers.

"They gave us loads of packages — food, water, toys — and took us to another bus," Iryna proceeds, "We were brought to a school converted into a makeshift refugee camp."

There, the family spent the night. The place was warm, and refugees had access to food and the Internet. There were also volunteer translators who provided important information on where to go next and where to find housing in Slovakia.

"This first encounter was warm, though a little intrusive," Iryna continues, "Several people asked me if I was hungry, and everyone tried to give my daughter gifts, even though her arms were already full."

Vlada, Iryna's daughter, did not understand what was happening: she still thinks that her mother and her are simply taking another vacation, a trip to a new country. For Iryna, the reality is very different.

"I had a feeling of being in some kind of a parallel universe," the woman says, "Now, I am homeless and depend on people around me. I even have to ask the family that adopted me for an extra T-shirt, so that I could finally sleep in clean clothing after three days of travel and taking breaks only to sleep."

Iryna hopes to go back to Ukraine soon, but she realizes it may not be possible.

"Those I managed to speak to at the border are not too optimistic that the war will end soon," the woman explains, "Many ask how we are doing. I have an answer for them: We are fighting! The Ukrainian military is superb, and Ukrainians are strong and united. Therefore, victory is close!"

Guilt and Anxiety about the Future

Many people feel guilt after fleeing Ukraine as they are forced to leave other relatives behind.

Olena Ocheredko, a volunteer on Moldovan border with Ukraine, says she needs to convince some women not to go back to Ukraine after they cross the border with their children.

"I try to convince them that they are where they are supposed to be," Olena says, "After all, their husbands can fight better knowing that their loved ones are safe. Many people spent days and nights in the basements without water and heating. If they stayed in Ukraine, they would be an extra liability for the defenders."

Olena herself is a Ukrainian who lives on the Moldovan-Ukrainian border. According to her, Ukrainians don't ask for anything luxurious as they flee the war. People are quite happy to get a roof over their heads and sleep without the fear of bombing.

A refugee who fled to Moldova and who prefers to stay anonymous also shares her story with me.

"I spent four days in a cold basement with my children," she confesses, "Our house was destroyed. My husband brought me to the border, and then he came back. My children and I went into the unknown. Volunteers picked us up in the middle of the night and brought us here."

Another refugee from Odesa gives a similar testimony.

"We are eight women and children," she says, "We grabbed only our passports and left the city. Our husbands stayed at home to fight. We wanted to remain in Ukraine, too, and now, some of our friends blame us for leaving."

"We Shouldn't Become a Battlefield Due to Your Silence!"

Testimonies from Two Different Women Named Yuliia — One in Kyiv and One in Vienna

March 2022

They are both Ukrainians, they are both volunteers, and they are both suffering. Both Yuliias are working to spread honest information about the war in Ukraine. Here are their thoughts:

Yuliia from Vienna

Hey everyone, my name is Yuliia. I come from the Western part of Ukraine, from the Carpathian Mountains, and I am currently studying at the Central European University in Vienna. I am in Vienna right now, and this is a very safe and privileged position to be in, as I was not impacted by the war as much as those in my country. Still, all my family is currently in Ukraine, doing their best to help host internally displaced people from other regions. In Vienna, we are also doing our best to support Ukraine from abroad; we are collecting humanitarian aid and civilian defense items, and we are supporting Ukraine on the information front. A couple of days ago, we started making a podcast highlighting the voices of real people from the war.

We've also opened a couple of centers where we are collecting humanitarian aid for the refugees already in Vienna and for those who are impacted by the war in Ukraine. We are trying to change the situation somehow. I guess that the information front is one of the most important fronts at the moment, as there is lots and lots of Russian propaganda that has impacted many Western countries, the Middle East and the world in general. So, one of our aims is to spread the truth and to help people in different regions know this truth.

I want to say that the war in Ukraine is a very, very nasty aggression on the part of Russia. This is the real face of Russian imperialism, which operates differently from the U.S. version. I really want people in the West, especially people who consider themselves leftist or some sort of leftist, to think more critically, to listen to our voices, and to understand that this war is not about them. This is about us.

This is about real aggression and real colonialism, which is happening in my land, and my people are impacted and being killed by Russian troops. Yes, we're doing our best to survive, and we will do our best to fight back and defend our territorial integrity, our democracy, and our people. But you should help us! Please, donate to our army, and please, please, demand that your government institute a no-fly zone over Ukraine. It is such a double standard that we are to be the battlefield for your silence. Thank you so much. And take care!

Yuliia from Mariupol/Kyiv

Hi all. My name is Yuliia Zahorodna. I am from Mariupol (currently occupied by Russians – AR), and now I live in Kyiv. I studied in Mariupol, and then I got my Master's degree in Media Communications from the Ukrainian Catholic University in Lviv. I currently work in the Press Office of Kyiv International Airport "Zhulyany."

What should people know about the Russian war in Ukraine? People need to know that we lost everything in the war, and I am not talking about material things. We have lost those close to us; we have lost our feelings—that's what happened to me. I completely lost my humanity and emotions toward those people who live in the invading country. I am not sorry for what is happening to them, and I am ready to attack them myself.

I am not sorry for what will happen to them in the next fifty years. I really want the worst things to happen to them for their silence. On the other hand, I understand that this is very bad because I am losing what makes me human and humane; I am losing human qualities. Be ready to lose all of that in war. You also lose your loved ones, your dreams, and yourself. It is very scary, and the scariest thing is what happens next. You don't know what will happen, and there is no exit. You don't know who you are going to be, how you are going to look, how you will behave and whether you will keep anything that you were before the war. It is a complete loss of oneself. I call on everyone who will hear me to think of this. Don't think about material things; think that you are losing everything that makes you human.

"Mom, When Are We Going Home?"

The Russian War Displaced More than Half of Ukraine's Children. Here's a Story of One

April 2022

"Don't be scared, she doesn't bite," I say, a little bit too reassuringly.

Deep inside, I know I am only telling half the truth, because I have no idea how Svitlana, our gigantic and spoiled bunny, will behave.

Svitlana is one of the pets we have on a farm in a small village in Western Ukraine. She is used to being arm-fed, and I hope this interests Il'ko, my little guest.

For a few minutes, it does not seem to work. Il'ko looks terrified by a giant bunny, and he does not understand if Svitlana will eat from my hand or will bite my finger off.

But then, something changes.

As Svitlana confidently grabs the carrot I offer, Il'ko smiles. His smile is shy at first, but then, it grows into a one big grin.

"She is so goofy," he manages to squeak in-between the laughs.

"Yes, she is. And she is also super big."

I encourage Il'ko to pet Svitlana, who, happy with her carrot, does not seem to mind. The boy gently puts his little arm on the white head and makes delicate movements.

"Woah," he exhales.

"Do you want to see more pets?" I ask.

He nods.

I do a little dance in my head: this is already going much better than our first encounter. So, I wink to Il'ko as we embark on a little trip around the farm. He seems excited.

"This Is Illya. I Mean, Il'ko"

I first met Il'ko two weeks ago when he and his family arrived to my apartment in a small town in Lviv oblast, a Western region in Ukraine that borders Poland.

The family, consisting of Il'ko, his parents, grandparents, and an aunt, traveled from Kyiv. The trip, which should normally take around seven hours, lasted two days. There was a huge traffic jam and a curfew, so cars could not move freely at night.

The areas around the capital have also seen some heavy fighting. As Russian troops tried to encircle Kyiv, they captured a few towns nearby where they massacred civilians.

"We decided we had to get out," says Sasha, Il'ko's father, "We didn't want to wait for Russians to come."

Sasha's parents live in Boryspil, which is around a thirty-minute drive from Kyiv. The town is home to Ukraine's biggest airport and is one of the many potential targets in the region. When the war started, Sasha reached out to his parents and asked them to come to Kyiv. From there, a large family started their way toward the West.

They were lucky because they left before heavy strikes destroyed many buildings in Kyiv. Still, they spent the first days of the war in a subway, hiding during the air raids.

"It was too hard to do that with a child. We didn't want him to experience all that," Sasha motions to his son.

"Illya, Illya, come here," he continues, "Say hello to people."

As the child shyly stands in front of us, the father corrects himself all of a sudden. "I mean, Il'ko. He is Il'ko".

This is funny, I think. Il'ko and Illya are the same names, just different versions. Il'ko is more common for Ukrainian speakers, though.

Sasha and his family are Russian speakers. All adults speak Ukrainian around us even though we never mentioned the language. Il'ko speaks Russian. He is only five, so he has not been to school yet, and he has not learned Ukrainian. Most Russian-speaking children start speaking Ukrainian through school.

My parents and I did not know Il'ko or his family before the war. They were not even remote acquaintances. But when the war started, housing became really scarce in Western Ukraine, a relatively safe haven for many Ukrainians.

As people started arriving in hundreds of thousands, many reached out to family members, friends, and colleagues to find a shelter. Il'ko's father knows my uncle, and through him, they found us.

My parents live on a farm, but they also own a small apartment in a town nearby. Now, this crammed two-bedroom is hosting six people of three generations.

"It Is Very Calm in Here"

"Your town is very lovely," says Lena, Sasha's wife and Il'ko's mother, "We walked around when we arrived, and we really enjoyed it. There is so much nature and quiet."

She is holding Il'ko's hand—the child is very quiet and shy. We call those "greenhouse kids" because they rarely get real-world experience. You can tell that Il'ko is really attached to his mother and that the war made him rely on her even more. He did not like the sirens in Kyiv, and he is worried to hear them here.

"Il'ko really liked the children's park you have," Lena continues as she strokes her son's head. She is a petite woman, blond like her son, with delicate hands. She is in her mid-thirties, and her husband is around forty. Lena used to work as an office manager in Kyiv, but she is unsure if she has a job anymore. Many companies have stopped working due to war.

Sasha is already retired. He is a pilot, but he has not flown in years—many leave work when they reach 35.

Sasha's parents, Nataliia and Volodymyr, are also retired. They are both in their seventies. There is also El'vira, Volodymyr's older sister. She is a widow and has no children.

"Thank you so, so much for having us," Nataliia keeps repeating.

Out of the entire family, she seems the most friendly and open as the rest is still traumatized from the war. She is very grateful—

in fact, too grateful, as she keeps on repeating how thankful she is for our house offer.

My parents and I are not used to this; my mom gently brushes her off.

"Don't mention it," she says, "It's what we all should do."

We don't stay long in the apartment—the point of our visit was to show what's where, help with any issues, and bring some food: my mom got a bag of potatoes for the family. My dad also exchanged numbers with Sasha because he's taking the man to the local city council. All internally displaced people in Ukraine have to register to receive help and for security reasons. All men, too, are required to report: they may be conscripted if the need arises.

"If you want, we have a farm nearby which you can visit," my mom offers, "In case you are bored and want to have a walk or something."

The grandparents seem to brighten up: they don't have much to do in a new town, so they happily agree. Sasha and Lena also nod: the farm may be fun for Il'ko.

Childhood Needs Protection

I didn't realize this at that time, but Il'ko has never been on a farm. Our bunnies were exotic animals to him. The child was scared of chickens and ran away from a rooster. I know it's mean to laugh at a five-year-old, but it was funny.

I think the animals did Il'ko well.

He forgot about the sirens because he has to face another threat: a bunch of angry birds.

"Don't worry, they are just chickens. They are not very clever, and they don't attack people," I say.

I am showing Il'ko the farm, but he seems a little nervous. On our drive here, I gave him a little toy car, but he barely touched it. I am very inexperienced with kids, so that was discouraging; but I also realize that he is a quiet and sensitive boy, and he was just displaced from his home, which is very traumatic. So I try harder to be nice.

"Do you want to see a bunny?" I ask.

And this is when the miracle happens. Svitlana breaks the ice. The chubby bunny has no idea of the effect she made on the child as he finally relaxes. I then introduce him to Barack, our other bunny, and although the pet does not seem to care about the kid too much, Il'ko looks genuinely amused.

"You see, Il'ko, when we are back, you can get yourself a cute pet like this one," says grandpa Volodymyr. Our farm reminds of his home in Boryspil, and he daydreams of returning.

"El'vira already wants to go back," he tells me with sadness in his voice, "But it is way too early. Right, boy?"

Il'ko winks at his grandpa as we walk around the house, the chickens, and the garden. The child starts to run around and does not mind me or others anymore. He seems happy, like an average five-year-old.

"You have such a lovely home," Nataliia reappears from the house as she chats with my mom. Lena and El'vira follow. The women were having cake while my dad was showing Sasha our garden. Grandpa Volodymyr joins them.

I am not quite sure how to call our new residents. They are not tenants because we don't rent our place to them; it's free. And they are not guests either. If it wasn't for the war, we'd probably never meet. Il'ko would not see any bunnies, and I would not worry about making him laugh. But here we are.

This is the reality of millions of Ukrainians affected by the war. More than 4.3 million of Ukrainian children have been displaced. More than a million left the country while others moved to Western regions with their families. Many don't go to school and are traumatized by what they saw in the war: bombs and deaths.

The story of Il'ko is, however, much better than of those who are still in Mariupol and other areas under Russian siege. It's true that Il'ko is not in his home, but he is with his family in a relative safety of Western Ukraine. Many children don't even get that.

Some are stuck in basements for weeks, without food, water, or heating. They cannot leave because the shelling does not stop. The invaders also target evacuation buses.

In the first month of the war, Russian troops killed at least 128 Ukrainian children.

A Story from a Russian Filtration Camp

"My Boyfriend and I Both Tried to Flee Mariupol," says Kateryna, "I Managed, and He Did Not"

May 2022

I write this on the 89th day of the Russian-Ukrainian war. Now, Kateryna is in a territory controlled by the Ukrainian government. Her boyfriend, Maksym, is in a Russian filtration camp, and is likely to stay there for long.

Kateryna and Maksym are both from Mariupol. There, she has been working for a local furniture company. Kateryna lived in the city with her parents while Maksym lived in another part of Mariupol, and they would commute to see each other.

Mariupol is one of the cities Russia nearly wiped out after its full-scale invasion of Ukraine. It borders the so-called Donetsk People's Republic, a territory in Eastern Ukraine occupied by Russia since 2014. Many Mariupol locals are used to hearing explosions nearby due to fighting between Ukrainian and Russian forces in the area. However, the city remained relatively calm until 2022.

It Was Impossible to Leave

"I was shaken when the full-scale invasion started," Kateryna says, "But I hoped for the best and didn't want to leave the city right away."

Her family stayed in Mariupol until mid-March.

"At first, we hid in our apartment, in the corridor where there are no windows, but it got too dangerous. We moved to the building basement after a few days," Kateryna recalls, "By early March, we didn't have electricity, heating, or running water anymore."

A house next to their building got bombed, and the family saw corpses on the street. This is when Kateryna and her family decided to flee.

"I called Maksym and told him my parents and I wanted to try to leave Mariupol," Kateryna recalls, "By that time, it was already very difficult to move around the city, and there was almost no gas."

Maksym said that he would try to reach their part of Mariupol so they all could leave together.

But Maksym could not show up because his area was bombed, and the movement was too deadly.

Kateryna's family had to go first. They left the basement and headed to the area near the Drama Theatre, where they tried to join an evacuation convoy that was about to leave the city. However, the evacuation was not successful.

"Ukrainian soldiers and volunteers told us it was too dangerous to go because Russians didn't agree to the green corridor," she recalls, "Russians kept on shooting at the cars, and it was impossible to leave."

"I Cannot Describe the Horror"

The family decided not to stay in their apartment; they went into one of the makeshift hospitals in the area that was used by the Ukrainian army. Kateryna's parents were already exhausted by that time, so they fainted and felt very weak. The hospital staff provided some help, but they could not attend to them much, given the number of wounded people pouring in.

"I went to check on our house a few times, but then, it didn't matter anymore," Kateryna says.

While she was staying in the hospital, her building alongside the entire street was completely destroyed.

"I know that there are some satellite images, but they don't really show what it was like," the woman recalls, "I cannot describe the horror of what we saw."

Kateryna remembers corpses on the streets and the utter devastation of the city she once called her home. She knew she could not stay in the hospital for long because it was only a matter of days until got destroyed, too.

In mid-March, Kateryna and her family managed to leave, "Our car still had some gas, and we joined the car convoy that was fleeing the city."

Russian forces still shot at some cars, but Kateryna's was spared.

"When we reached the first Ukrainian checkpoint, I started crying," Kateryna says, "I could finally breathe freely."

The Prison-like Filtration Camp

However, when Kateryna was leaving Mariupol, she didn't know what was happening with Maksym. This is because most of the telecommunications infrastructure had been damaged, and it was also difficult to find a place to charge one's phone.

Kateryna is now in Western Ukraine, in relative safety. Her family is with her. She tried to contact Maksym, but he was out of reach, so she got in touch with his mother. From her, she learned that Maksym was taken to a village around 50 kilometers from Mariupol by the Russian forces. As Russians gained more and more control over the city districts, they were able to capture most people who stayed behind. Many women and children were deported to Russia, and men were taken to Russia-controlled areas in the so-called Donetsk People's Republic.

Later, it was actually Maksym who connected with her by Instagram text.

Maksym told Kateryna that he was staying in a school in the occupied territory and that the building was now serving as a prison to keep the men from Mariupol captive.

"Maksym reached me in the middle of April as he managed to connect to wi-fi in that school," Kateryna explains, "He said there were nearly 200 people with him, all men from Mariupol, whose passports were taken away. All had the same story as him: they stayed in the city until it was too difficult to get evacuated, and then the Russians took them. Most men also had to give away their phones, so Maksym was luckier."

Maksym told Kateryna that he was not beaten up, but he has seen men who were tortured and covered in bruises. Many men were sick and did not receive medication. There were men with chronic diseases, and some men also got covid or covid-like symptoms — even though it was impossible to know for sure as no medic ever inspected them.

"He has been texting me every day, sometimes calling although it was risky, so he didn't do it often," Kateryna says, "He told me he was hungry because they didn't get a lot of food, and its quality was bad."

Maksym also told her that they didn't have any shower rooms, so they could only wash in a sink in the general bathroom. He said that he knew some men tried to run away but failed. They were later taken away, and the guards told them they went to "Isolation" in Donetsk. This is a torture chamber.

"I called the official number of Donetsk People's Republic to ask about Maksym, but the person on the line told me that the man with his passport was already released," Kateryna says helplessly, "So I don't know what else to do."

Maksym is among more than a million of Ukrainians displaced from Ukraine to Russia-controlled areas. He has been held captive for more than a month. Russia refuses to release him or other captives.

A Journey beyond the Carpathians

Southwestern Part of the Country Offers Some Sort of Normalcy despite the War

May 2022

"What are we, not Ukrainians? We've got the same problems as you guys!"

That's Vita, a shopkeeper from Uzhorod. The city is the capital of Zakarpattya, Ukraine's most Western region. Vita is a bit annoyed as she walks me through the local street life.

"It doesn't matter if we're far from the border," she says, "We suffer, too!"

A moment ago, I asked her if she felt more secure in her home than, let's say, Ukrainians living in the capital, Kyiv. For Vita, the question was silly.

"Of course, we worry! Russian missiles are Russian missiles, they target us just fine, you know!" the woman grunts.

But then, a small smile appears on her face.

"I mean, we are much better now than during the first days of the invasion. Nobody runs to the shelter anymore," Vita talks slowly, "We figured that nobody is safe, but we can try to live through it."

A Borderland

Vita is nearing fifty. She was born and raised in Zakarpattya. This southwestern region is conveniently located right next to the NATO borders: it takes you less than an hour to get to Romania, Hungary, Slovakia, or Poland from here.

Zakarpattya has suffered from Russian attacks, but less than the rest of Ukraine. There were missile strikes that hit local infrastructure and train facilities, so some people are afraid of traveling by train. But besides that, the region has been spared so far.

When I arrive here, I am surprised at how nearly normal everything looks. There are checkpoints on the main streets, and there are more military men, but the rest of the local reality is very similar to how it was before Russia's full-scale invasion of Ukraine.

Zakarpattya is the only region in the country that does not have a curfew. You can drive here freely after 10 in the evening. There are people on the streets at night and some social events; the nearby town of Uzhorod is hosting a charity marathon to raise funds for the army. This reminds me of the pre-war days.

Vita notes that business is doing okay, too, given the situation. People don't buy as many clothes now because of the war — many try to save some money for their unclear future. But she still manages to make ends meet.

Before the war, Vita and her husband routinely traveled to Hungary to buy clothing, which they would later sell in Ukraine. She travels less now and only by herself because her husband cannot leave Ukraine — this rule applies to most Ukrainian men under 60 as they may potentially be needed for the army.

Vita is of Hungarian origin, but even though she grew up speaking Hungarian, she never taught her husband or her two daughters the language.

"What are we, not Ukrainians?" she repeats herself.

Zakarpattya is Ukraine's most ethnically diverse region; while the majority are Ukrainians, there is a large percentage of people with Hungarian, Romanian, Slovak, Jewish, and Romani roots. People speak a mix of different languages, but Ukrainian remains the lingua franca.

As for Vita, she says that she feels Ukrainian, and so does her family. They never considered moving to the EU, even when the invasion started.

"We are from Zakarpattya, and we are not going anywhere, war or no war," she reasons.

"You Cannot Forget the War Even If You Don't See It Right Away"

I am at a gas station in Mukachevo, the second-largest city in Zakarpattya. It is almost midnight, but there are lots of people here. Without a curfew, people drive freely during late hours, and the café at a gas station is full of customers.

The city center, however, reminds me that there is a war in the country. It is dark and pretty quiet for a summer night; the streetlights are turned off for security reasons. People can go out, but they are encouraged to do so in small groups and remain calm and civil. Parties are frowned upon even here.

"There is no curfew, but it's not like people go dancing all night," says Andriy, a Mukachevo local. He is a former journalist who now works as a translator.

"People want to go out and relax, but it's tricky. You see, there are folks who want to pretend that there is no war, but everyone has someone who is currently fighting, so you cannot really forget about it, however peaceful it may feel here," the man says.

Andriy points out to me that the city has changed more than I noticed: for example, there are no concerts and festivals taking place now, and even on holidays, there are no celebrations. There is a large volunteer mobilization because Zakarpattya is an important hub for humanitarian aid coming in from the West. In addition, people became more attentive and observe their neighbors and new arrivals.

"Everyone is looking out for spies and potential saboteurs from Russia," the man says.

With Andriy, we visit AwareZone, Mukachevo's first collaborative workspace. It is the city's pride as it was opened by internally displaced people. The space, launched at the end of June, aims to bring together locals and new arrivals so people can exchange and get to know each other better.

"When I came to Mukachevo, local youth told me that they had no place to meet. We knew right away that there was a space for work," says Yuriy Davydenko. He is a project manager behind the hub who came to Mukachevo after the start of the full-scale invasion.

Yuriy is originally from Mariupol, in Eastern Ukraine, which is now nearly destroyed by Russian forces. Back in Mariupol, the man has launched a successful coworking space, so he decided to do the same in his new home.

"In a month, we created a new hub for developing startups and meeting the activists. My experience from Mariupol really helped me here," Yuriy says, "Now, we've got the hardest task to complete, which is to fill this space with life and to create an ecosystem so people would come and be active here."

Zakarpattya welcomed around 300,000 internally displaced people (IDP), which is a quarter of the entire population of the region. Many IDPs are here to stay as their homes were destroyed, and they have nowhere else to go — so they are looking for housing to buy in the region as well as seeking long-term employment. The newcomers are slowly adapting to life here and praise the relative security and calmness in their new region.

The location of Zakarpattya, its proximity to the NATO and EU borders, and its mountainous landscape make it a safer haven than the rest of Ukraine. Now the question arises of how to integrate the internally displaced in the country's most ethnically diverse region.

Ukrainians Return Home, but Fear Remains

The Number of People Returning to Ukraine Is Far Greater than Those Leaving Now

June 2022

Blue-and-yellow flags are everywhere, along with stickers and announcements in Ukrainian. This is how Warsaw greets me. The capital of Poland has become an important city for Ukrainians fleeing the war. Located only four hours away from the Polish-Ukrainian border, Warsaw is a temporary home for hundreds of thousands of refugees.

Warsaw's train and bus stations are still full of signs and stands for Ukrainians. There are volunteers who can explain to new arrivals how to get help, and there are guidelines on how to get free food and housing.

However, the influx of people is significantly smaller now. When in February and March, Warsaw — as well as other Polish cities — felt like they were going to explode from this flow, the situation has now stabilized. There are still tens of thousands of new residents from Ukraine staying across the city, but they have managed to adapt and adjust for the time being. There are also a few Ukrainians who came to Poland in May.

"Ukrainians are welcome here, and we understand that if something like this happened to us, they would welcome us," says Malgorzata, a Warsaw local. She has been volunteering for Ukrainians, donating food to them, and offering a spare room in her apartment to a Ukrainian family for free. The family left two weeks ago.

"It was a little bit difficult," she recalls, "The woman was very nice, but the child had a disability, so it was very difficult to transport him and explain to him why they were not in Ukraine. He always wanted to return."

Malgorzata says that she understands Ukrainians who are already going back home and thinks they are very brave.

"I think it is very scary to be somewhere where bombs are falling on you," she reasons, "But home is home, and nothing is like that."

Malgorzata and I are sitting in a café in an upper-middle-class district on the outskirts of Warsaw. It is about a thirty-minute drive from the city center, and there is nothing that gives away that we are in the capital of a country. It is a very calm and quiet neighborhood, full of residential areas, greenery, and places to eat out.

As we walk the streets, Ukrainian flags pop out everywhere. When I order or ask questions in Ukrainian, Poles answer me in Polish, having understood my language perfectly. This impresses me.

"A lot of people are now using Duolingo to learn some Ukrainian," Malgorzata smiles, "I did too. The languages are already quite similar, but this helped me communicate."

"I Don't Have Illusions about Anything"

As I prepare to depart from the city, I order an Uber to take me to a bus station conveniently located ten minutes away, near the airport.

I notice that my driver, quiet at first, uses Google Maps in Ukrainian. We start talking.

"I don't know if I will stay here for long, but in terms of quality of life and price, Warsaw is not bad at all," Yuriy, the driver, says. He has been here since before Russia's full-scale invasion. Initially, he was doing seasonal work and coming back to Ukraine after each season. When Russia attacked, he decided to stay in Poland.

"And you, why are you going back to Ukraine?" he asks.

I explain to him that I don't live in Poland, and I was there just for a day for work.

"I see," Yuriy becomes pensive, "Well, I don't know if I will go back. I was considering going to Canada or somewhere in the US."

I tell him that life there is very expensive and not as shiny as we may think.

"I know all of that, I do," he dismisses my comment, "I don't have those rose-colored glasses anymore. I lost my illusions a long time ago. It's just that I don't want to be in Europe anymore. I am sick of it."

Yuriy is from the southwest of Ukraine, as I can hear from his accent. He is here with his wife, renting an apartment and working as a cab driver.

"I admire you for going back," he says as I leave the car, almost apologetically.

As I get off, I am greeted by the Chopin airport, the largest in Poland. It has a big Ukrainian flag next to the Polish one. I remember a few Polish words and ask an airport employee how to get to the buses. It is a one-minute walk.

"I Couldn't Stay Away Anymore"

The bus is full. I chose the more expensive one, with air conditioning and Internet, although the latter does not work. A passenger next to me tells me that there are buses to Ukraine every hour, as well as trains and other means to get to the border. It appears that all passengers are Ukrainians going home.

"I haven't been to Ukraine for three months," Nadia, a woman next to me, says. She is in her early thirties and looks stern and nervous.

"I debated for a long time whether to go or not, and here I am," the passenger adds.

Nadia's parents never left Ukraine, but she was outside of the country when the full-scale invasion occurred.

"I was on vacation in Egypt when all of it happened," she recalls, "My friend and I were in shock. We didn't know what to do. At first, the Ukrainian embassy was paying for our stay, but after a few weeks, they asked us to find something cheaper or to use one of the evacuation planes to go to Europe."

So, Nadia flew to Germany at first. There, she stayed with her acquaintance, and in May, she moved to Poland.

"I volunteered both in Germany and Poland, helping people, translating, and so on," she says, "But I was growing restless, and I could not stay abroad anymore."

Nadia is from Zaporizhzhia, a city very close to the frontline. It is in the south of Ukraine, and Russians have occupied some parts of this region in their attempt to control access to the Ukrainian seas.

"My parents tell me that there are air sirens pretty much every day," the woman says, "But I miss them too much, and I miss home. I think I don't understand the war because I have only seen it on TV, but I hope I can be useful there."

During a short break, I strike up a conversation with another passenger, a girl named Yuliia. She looks very young, almost like a minor.

"I'm actually twenty-four, but I've been asked that a lot," she laughs when I question her age and how she is traveling by herself.

"I've been in and out of Poland twice," she says, "The first time, I helped transport my cousin, who has cerebral palsy and couldn't stay in Ukraine under these conditions. The second time was this week because I came to visit him and his mom."

Yuliia tells me that none of her friends have left, and most of her family has stayed in Ukraine too. The only people who are abroad are the ones who had health problems and couldn't receive treatment in Ukraine anymore.

"I never even thought about leaving," she continues, "Maybe it's because I'm from Lviv, and we feel like the front line is a bit further, or maybe it's just that I never imagined myself away from Ukraine for long."

Yuliia works for an IT company; she volunteers in her home city and plans to keep it that way until Ukraine wins.

"I hope all Ukrainians who are abroad will come back when we win," the woman concludes, "We will need a lot of people to rebuild everything."

As we approach the Polish-Ukrainian border, I can see that we will have to wait for a long time: there is a long line of cars and buses on their way to Ukraine and no cars heading toward Poland. We stand for four hours in between the countries until we finally get our passports stamped.

On average, around 70,000 Ukrainians return home per day, and nearly 5 million Ukrainian refugees have already come back to their country after spending some time in safer European countries. This represents 60% of all refugees who fled Ukraine, and more keep going back.

"LGBT Ukrainians Can Defend Themselves"

A Story of a Bisexual Sniper in the Ukrainian Army

July 2022

"Bisexuality was always with me: when I was a child, I thought that everyone was like me, and that everyone liked both girls and boys. As a teen, I learned that it was called bisexuality."

This is I., a 26-year-old soldier serving in Ukraine's Armed Forces. She joined the army years before the full-scale invasion, training to be a paramedic and then a sniper. I. prefers to keep her identity hidden until Ukraine wins the war. She says it's easier that way.

Here's her story.

"I Never Planned to Join the Military"

"I never had any problems with relationships nor with how others perceived me," I. says, "I am very creative and communicative."

Before joining the army, the girl studied philology and worked as an editor and an artist. Then, as she graduated from the university, she decided to go to the East to volunteer. At that time the war in Donbas started when Russian forces occupied parts of Eastern Ukraine and also, annexed the Crimean Peninsula. In Donbas, I. served as a paramedic.

"It is normal: when your country is in danger, you contribute regardless of the fact that you never planned to join the military," she says.

After several years of volunteering, I. signed a contract. By then, she finished her training as a combat medic and went on rotation with her first unit. She was serving at the Donetsk region, the one on the frontline.

"Obviously, the people in the unit were different," I. says, "Besides me, there were two lesbian girls in the battalion. Everyone treated them well, and they treated me the same way. I didn't hide my sexual orientation, although I didn't particularly emphasize it.

It was my naivety that led to a very unpleasant story related to all this."

Ukraine, like many countries across the world, celebrates the day against homophobia on May 17. On that day, one of the Ukrainian media reached out to I. and asked for a commentary. A journalist was writing a story on whether there was any discrimination in the army due to sexual orientation.

"I responded honestly: I sent a few phrases like that I didn't experience any discrimination, everything was good, and I could gossip with boys about girls," I. recalls, "The story got published, and I shared it on my Facebook page."

This is when the issues began.

"The unit leader read the story first, and my position commander got verbally reprimanded for my interview," I. recalls, "Then, we got a visit from the battalion commander's deputy, who arrived at our position. He told me to contact him in case I had any problems with bullying or if someone made fun of me. He also told me I should have coordinated this interview with the press service. The deputy was right because I should have done that first, but I didn't want to bother the press officer for nothing. I figured that my short comment, focused solely on me, was not important enough to involve a press officer."

The soldier's comrades split over her media statement.

"One group was super against me, full of offended jackasses, and the others had more important things to worry about," I. explains, "The unit leader decided to support the jackasses, so he sent me from the position into the rear. I learned that it happened because of my interview because my friends asked my unit leader and sergeants about it."

Nobody openly said anything to I. though. The official explanation was that it was necessary for her to get back to the rear even though the girl had nothing to do with the new post.

"LGBT People in Ukraine Need the Law"

"I don't know how long I would have stayed in this position, but I reached out to the people higher in command and explained the whole situation to them," I. proceeds, "I had nothing to lose, and I hinted that I could give another interview, which would not be so innocent this time. After a few hours, I was returned to my previous position and duties, and nobody said a thing. But I didn't say anything publicly about LGBT either. It was a kind of unspoken compromise."

A year later, the girl decided to change her profession. She switched units and learned how to be a sniper. When the full-scale Russian invasion happened, I. remained in her unit, fighting against a much bigger force.

"In my new unit, only two people I trust the most know about my sexual identity. I don't want to risk anything or get into discussions with fellow soldiers because what I do is very important to me," I. says.

The girl hopes that Ukraine will legalize LGBT marriages soon and that this will change how the community is perceived across the country.

In July, a petition to legalize same-sex marriages gathered 25,000 signatures, which is enough to pass it to the Ukrainian President for review. It took Ukrainians around one month to get the needed amount of signatures.

By the end of July, Zelenskyy will have to respond to the petition. The President can determine whether to forward it to the parliament so they can draft the new law.

"LGBT people in Ukraine need the law," I. says, "Thank God, the discrimination is already legally punishable. When we legalize same-sex marriages, the conservatives will complain a bit, but they will quickly get used to it."

"What's another thing LGBT Ukrainians need?" I. reasons, "Well, we need to kick the Russians out. In Russia, LGBT people are either dead, or exiled, or sit quietly like a mouse under the broom."

"LGBT Ukrainians can defend themselves, and they are doing that successfully," the soldier concludes.

In the last six years, Ukraine has seen a significant improvement in attitudes toward LGBT. In 2016, there were more than 60% of Ukrainians who felt negative toward LGBT; now, this number is

38%. The amount of people with a positive attitude toward LGBT grew from 3.3% in 2016 to 12.8% in 2022. Most Ukrainians remain indifferent: around 45%.

The attitudes change with age: senior citizens are the least receptive toward LGBT, while youth under 29 is most open and tolerant.

According to "Nash Svit," an LGBT Human Rights Center, the start of the Russian invasion of Ukraine in 2014 marked a major shift in Ukrainian society. As Ukrainians increasingly supported greater European integration, they also became more responsive to LGBT rights, and LGBT movements received wider coverage. There is a constant increase in violence toward the LGBT community, and there are openly gay soldiers and public figures. However, problems remain. Activists emphasize the need to legislate equal marriage, investigate hate crimes, and normalize battling everyday homophobia.

Surviving the Russo-Ukraine war with Disability

An Activist Shares Her First-Hand Account

August 2022

"When my mom told me that the invasion started, I had no other option than leave," Tetiana Herasymova explained, "It was a no-brainer."

She said it matter-of-factly, with a hint of sadness in her voice.

"I knew that for me, there was no going back, and I had to make that transition," the woman continued, "If I didn't leave right away, I would never leave."

Tetiana Herasymova—or Tania, for short—is an activist. She is a project coordinator at Ukraine's Fight for Right, an NGO that advocates for the rights of people with disabilities.

When Russia launched its full-scale invasion against Ukraine, Herasymova's organization added a new, very important project, to its portfolio: evacuating disabled people trapped in the war zone. In less than five months, the team rescued more than two thousand people. Requests for rescue keep coming—there are more than a thousand pending.

"Everything was very chaotic in the beginning, and we didn't announce that we were evacuating anyone," Herasymova said, "But we saw that nobody else was doing it, so we had to fill the gap."

"I Did Not Want to Leave"

"I use a wheelchair, and I am from Kamianske in the Dnipro region," Herasymova began.

She is a young woman in her early thirties, with bright red hair and a friendly face.

"I was preparing for the full-scale war, so I had my emergency suitcase ready," the activist continued, "When my mom woke me up on February 24, saying that the invasion started, I knew we had to leave."

Herasymova used to live with her mother on the fourth floor of an apartment building. Her native Kamianske is less than three-hour drive from the Donetsk region, where the fighting between Russian and Ukrainian forces has been heaviest. The city, with its more than 200,000 residents, does not have a single bomb shelter that is accessible for wheelchair users. Herasymova knows this because she asked the city council. Many locals who live with a disability didn't have that information—it was not widely communicated.

"My danger level was that I could either stay in my apartment for good or manage to get into a bomb shelter and sit there until the end of the war," Herasymova said.

Her mother, who also lives with a disability, moves around with crutches. It was difficult for both women to get out of the city and reach safety. On February 25, a second day after the invasion, they managed to get on a train going to Lviv, a large center in Ukraine's very West. The journey took 22 hours. The train was overcrowded and completely dark.

"It was before the panic reached its peak, but the fear was spreading quickly," Herasymova said. A few days later, it became nearly impossible to find train seats, as there were too many people trying to flee the East and move West.

In Lviv, Herasymova's friends met her and drove her to the Ukrainian-Polish border. The queue to get to the other side was around 20 kilometers long, and people could only move during the day. Herasymova's friends had to go back to the city, so the woman and her mom spent the night in a van of a stranger who agreed to let them in.

"In the morning, we saw that the line moved by less than a kilometer," she recalled, "It was impossibly slow."

Herasymova asked another man, a local volunteer, to help them cross into Poland. At first, he refused, but he later changed his mind. "The man came back to pick us up and told us he'd try to drive against the flow to get us closer to the checkpoint,"

Herasymova said, "He dropped us at another border, the one you cross on foot, and it was not crowded. I could not believe my eyes."

"I didn't have anyone in Poland or elsewhere, but my friends from Fight for Right told me that before I even leave Ukraine, there will already be somebody waiting for me in Poland," the woman recalled, "And that's how it was. They found volunteers who helped me in Poland, and later, they found people who helped me reach Denmark. That's where I am right now."

"I did not want to leave, and if I didn't cross the border back then, I would have stayed," she said.

Staying, however, would have been difficult even in Western Ukraine. The entire country has only two shelters that are wheelchair accessible: one in Lviv, and one in Dnipro. The shelters tend to be full due to high demand. Many disabled people have to be carried to get inside regular shelters, and then, they cannot leave or even use the bathroom as everything is built with able-bodied people in mind.

"This Is War. Evacuations Are Unpredictable"

"We started preparing for war three weeks before the full-scale invasion happened," Herasymova remembered, "Worrying news kept on coming, so we began collecting data on what people with disabilities should do in crises, how to help, how to avoid catastrophes, and what the law says on all of that. We learned that it's bad, not just in Ukraine, but everywhere because there was little information on how to protect disabled people."

The team decided to act even before the invasion actually happened. Before the war, Fight for Right was doing mostly advocacy work such as defending the rights of people with disabilities, pushing for a more accessible infrastructure and related legislation, and empowering disabled Ukrainians through education and networking. The invasion halted many of these activities.

"Even before the full-scale war, we launched a campaign on GoFundMe to raise money to provide psychological support for people with disabilities," Herasymova explained, "We opened a hotline so people could reach a psychologist, and we got huge support of more than 6.5 thousand donations from all over the world."

With more donations and support from international partners, Fight for Right started looking into how else they could help disabled Ukrainians.

"At the beginning of the war, we saw that there was nobody doing evacuations, which meant that people were not cared for by the state," Herasymova sighed, "We had to fill that gap. Otherwise, people would die."

With colleagues in different parts of Ukraine and the world, the organization started accepting evacuation requests. People could reach the team via phone or email, describe their situation and their needs, and then, either Fight for Right would set up an evacuation or send some other support. It was not always possible to set up rescues because some areas were inaccessible due to heavy fighting, and sometimes, people would change their minds and decide not to evacuate.

"People are scared and take a long time to decide," Herasymova explained, "They worry about accessibility of their new home, and people with mental disabilities struggle with being in crowded shelters."

Evacuations are complicated to coordinate because you need to find a moment when it's safe to leave, and waiting for this window of opportunity can take weeks. There is also a need to find suitable transportation, which can be especially tricky when evacuating large groups. Herasymova and her team had to rescue from 10 to 30 people at once—anything larger would not have been feasible for the NGO. These large evacuations are exceptions: Fight for Right focuses on helping and accompanying individuals.

"It is very difficult because you'd need to have some state support like an international agreement on where to transport the evacuees and where to host them," Herasymova said, "We can help evacuees find housing and get rehabilitation, but the responsibility of restarting their lives in a new place is on them."

Herasymova explained that most Ukrainians evacuated themselves, with little state intervention or help, especially in the beginning of the invasion. With time, evacuations became more organized, yet the priority has always been women with children. "There are some state-led evacuations of children from the institutions, but almost none for adults in mental institutions," Herasymova continued, "People with disabilities are forgotten by the state and big international organizations, which should be paying attention to this problem and working on it."

"We cannot evacuate everyone," the activist said, "We had situations when we did not manage to evacuate people because we got too many requests at once from really hot spots. We also suffered when our volunteers got killed on the route to evacuate others."

"This is war. Every evacuation is unpredictable," she adds, "You cannot prepare for everything. Right now, we can evacuate people from the Donetsk region, and we are very happy for that."

"We Should Not Rebuild as Before. We Should Rebuild Better and More Inclusive"

Five months into the invasion, the team improved its evacuation scheme. With more than forty regular volunteers as well as a network of those who can help from time to time, it has gotten easier to coordinate the work. Now, the organization's nearly 20 employees are getting back to other projects, such as promoting accessibility and defending the rights of disabled people in Ukraine.

"We are members of working groups on Ukraine's reconstruction, where we talk with the government about what we need," Herasymova says, "People with disabilities have to speak for themselves because nobody else can decide what is best for us. When we hear about inclusion and participation, it is normally from people without disability who don't include us and make decisions alone."

When Herasymova and her colleagues participate in government meetings, they lobby for greater inclusion and accessibility. There is a great disparity when it comes to representation because people with disabilities tend to be overlooked by decision-makers. In Ukraine, more than 2.7 million people have a disability, but that rarely translates into political power.

"We have few people with disabilities who become decision makers and politicians because it is a long competition, and you are often not perceived seriously," Herasymova explains, "There is a problem with institutions because it is easier to keep people with disabilities away so they would not have access to good education, and this excludes lots of people. A person with a disability has to work three times as hard to get an education and a job. Every life stage eliminates more and more people who could not fight until a certain objective."

Herasymova hopes that after the war, there will be a push for a more inclusive Ukraine because before, the disability issue was nearly invisible.

"Now that we are talking about Ukraine's reconstruction, it is very sad that disabilities are not present in all topics and subjects," Herasymova said, "We should not rebuild what we had before, no! We have to rebuild a new Ukraine which is friendly and accessible for all. If we do this from the start, we will not need to change things later on."

"For example, if we build a town, it has to be accessible," she said, "If there is an evacuation, we have to understand that there will be people with disabilities among the evacuees. We need to support people with disability who cannot leave the house. All of this has to be thought through. We need to involve people with disabilities on all stages and include communities from across Ukraine."

For Herasymova, disability representation is not just about one problem. It is a complex issue that needs the state, civil society, and average Ukrainians to work together – and recognize the need to care for and empower all citizens.

"We have to talk about disabilities from a very young age," Herasymova concluded, "And we have to move away from Soviet traditions of locking disabled people up. Ukraine is an EU member state now, so we should do better and build better for all."

Ukraine's Digital Front Works 24/7

Digital Volunteers Debunk False Russian Narratives about the Russian war

August 2022

Many of them have never met in real life; some went to the same university, and others share friends in common. Those are Ukraine's digital volunteers: an increasingly growing community of journalists, translators, designers, and experts in the creative sector.

"When Russia invaded Ukraine, I felt powerless. I couldn't fight, and I don't know anything else but writing," says Mariia, a digital volunteer. "But then, I realized that writing was my power."

Mariia is a communication expert from Lviv, Western Ukraine. She teaches organizations how to deliver their messages effectively and reach the largest audiences. Now, she is communicating Ukraine to the world and helping foreigners make sense of what is happening in the country.

"You may think that after a very obvious Russian invasion, the world would become immune to Russian propaganda," the expert says. "But Kremlin media narratives work in many mysterious ways."

Mariia highlights that even though both Ukrainians and Westerners are now less vulnerable to some of the Russian fakes, they still retransmit a lot of the lies the Kremlin spreads.

"Ukraine gave up its nuclear weapons thirty years ago, but Russia is now saying that we have nukes. I mean, it is completely absurd, but people do repeat it," she sighs.

Kremlin propaganda remains quite effective because it is shared so often. Even when media and experts debunk it, they still quote the lies, thus helping them spread. Digital volunteers try to change that.

"We aim to communicate Ukraine on Ukraine's terms—using only verified information," Mariia adds. "And we never repeat or quote Putin or his cronies. He is already quoted everywhere."

Marta Datsyuk is another digital volunteer. A graduate of Ukrainian Catholic University in Lviv, she studied and worked in media and communications.

"When Russian troops started their full-scale invasion into Ukraine, I didn't realize what was happening right away," the woman says. "Just like many others, I had many feelings, but I always try to keep my mind calm and collected."

Marta received an invite from her former university professor to join a platform that explains the war to foreigners—a place where people translate Ukrainian reality into many different languages and contexts.

"Now, I am doing whatever I can to be the most useful for my country," Marta explains. "I am in contact with Ukrainian and foreign journalists, I do translations, I produce stories and audio, and I also support Ukrainians who had to flee their homes."

Being a digital volunteer means doing a lot of research and monitoring. It also means analyzing what people outside of Ukraine write about ongoing events. Often, they ask questions on social media that are not answered by their national outlets. So, volunteers try to collect relevant data and make it accessible to all—by producing posters, visuals, infographics, and text-like stories.

Marta, Mariia, and other volunteers launched a platform that explains the Russian war in twenty languages.

Similar initiatives have appeared across the Ukrainian internet. Yuliia Mendel, a former press secretary of President Volodymyr Zelenskyy, launched a platform called "Ukraine Verified" to connect Western journalists with relevant and reliable sources. The Lviv Media Forum, Ukraine's largest media event, is now hosting journalists from all over Ukraine in Lviv and connecting Western media makers with fixers and locals across the country.

In addition to journalists, designers, and translators are working on the digital front. Oleksandra is an artist from Lviv. She now creates daily infographics and visuals that explain the Russian war in pictures.

"My work calms me down. Whenever I design something, I feel like I am contributing a tiny drop to Ukraine's victory," she says. "I feel like I am communicating the reality with numbers and truth."

Prior to the war, Oleksandra worked as a freelancer and had many orders from businesses in her native Lviv and across Ukraine. Now, she has no time for paid work.

"I am currently living off my savings so I can volunteer full-time," the woman says. "I don't know how long I can do that, but I can always freelance more if I run out of money."

Oleksandra remains optimistic regardless of the situation.

"In many ways, I am used to this type of work. As a freelancer, I never got to see my colleagues anyway, and now, it is just a bigger team and a much more important cause," she says. "I have never worked this much, to be honest, but it is the only thing that overcomes my anxiety."

Mariia, too, says her work makes her feel more hopeful.

"Reality is gloomy in Ukraine as we see Russian terrorism unfold in real life," she explains. "I feel a million different moods throughout the day, from absolute agony to actual hope."

"So, whenever I translate something into English, or publish verified data for Finnish audiences, or comment on the Russian propaganda for a Dutch newspaper, I feel like I help make a difference," Mariia concludes. "I don't think it is enough because it can never be, but I still do it."

"War or No War, We Have to Teach"

Ukrainian Educators Seek New Ways to Keep Their Students Learning

September 2022

Halyna is fifty. She has been teaching for almost thirty years in a small village school in the Lviv region. Throughout her career, she moved from a math teacher to Vice Principal, and she has also been an active organizer of extracurricular activities.

Halyna learned how to use Zoom, lead remote classes, and record videos during the pandemic. Now, she has to change her work once again because of the war.

"Children need school more than ever, especially when everyone is on edge. They need to be active," says Halyna.

"Education Is No Longer a Priority"

The teacher looks tired and does not want her pictures taken. Her face is stern and worried. Halyna is short and extremely skinny.

"The stress is eating me up," she manages a joke.

Halyna's school is small by Ukrainian standards, with around 150 students aged from 6 to 17. Many combine classes with the traditional village life routine: helping around small farms, gardening, and taking care of animals.

Most of Halyna's students remain in Ukraine and are keen to resume classes. During the first days of the war, the schools switched to an online model, but after one week, those in Western Ukraine returned to an offline mode. The same goes for schools in territories that are relatively calm, meaning there are no immediate Russian attacks.

Nearly 3 million children returned to classes as of March 21. Around 45 thousand of them are internally displaced — they fled their homes and are now living in another part of Ukraine. The Lviv region, where Halyna is based, received the most of such students — nearly 11 thousand.

For those who cannot go to classes physically, the Ministry of Education launched an online initiative. Classes are now shown on YouTube, via state educational platforms, and on national TV channels, so children can watch them however they can.

"The Ministry told us that we should be prepared to teach online if the students leave — or if we choose to leave," Halyna explains, "But I don't intend to flee Ukraine now, and I can't imagine teaching when I am in another country."

Her village started getting air alarms five days ago. Before, the sound system either did not work or there was no missile threat. Now, the alarms go off as often as five times a day.

"The sound is bearable, but the announcement is too heavy," the teacher continues, "I can only imagine how bad it is for the children to hear it four or five times a day."

She says that the students complain they cannot sleep well because the sirens often go off around five or six in the morning.

"We try to accommodate everyone in school," Halyna explains, "We have longer breaks, move around, and even sing songs just to distract ourselves."

Her school did not receive any children who were internally displaced so far, but she is expecting some will join later.

"We are almost at the end of the school year," the educator continues, "I don't know what will happen to seniors with the exams and everything, but if we get any new students, we will do what we can to help them."

Halyna's village is small and quite far from big cities, airports, or military bases. So, people feel relatively secure there, despite the sirens. Some parents have joined the army, while others are in territorial defense or volunteering elsewhere. Most locals try to keep on living as they did before the war.

"Soon, the planting season will start, and the children will have double work," Halyna explains, "They will need to study in school, and they will help their parents in the field. Many are now unsure if they can continue studying after graduation, so they worry less about their grades and care more about doing some work in the village or beyond."

"But I still prioritize education for them," the teacher continues, "I remind my students that the war will end, and they will leave the village at some point to go to universities and colleges. So, they cannot just live through the war as if there is no tomorrow."

"I get that nobody is planning ahead anymore," she concludes, "However after it is over, we will need to educate youth to help rebuild everything. War or no war, we have to teach so we have someone smarter than us to carry on."

She looks more tired as she says it, but she also manages to smile for the first time during our talk.

"I Try to Make My Students Laugh and Remain Hopeful"

Lyubov is a teacher of Ukrainian language and literature. She started her career right before the collapse of the Soviet Union. She recalls how different education was back then and now.

"We had to keep quiet on so many things," she says, "There were so many topics that were left unspoken."

For example, the students could only learn about Ukrainian writers who were "approved" by the Soviet regime. Most works were banned as "nationalist" and not "socialist enough".

"I remember that the teachers of Russian language and literature would get an extra salary, and we didn't," Lyubov continues, "That was Soviet-style education."

When Ukraine became independent, many things changed. The Ukrainian language became a priority: now every student has to pass a language test after graduation. It is a prerequisite for applying to university.

"We saw a resurrection of interest toward our language and literature," Lyubov says, "We could finally teach the students about the persecution of Ukrainian writers by the Soviets and during the Russian empire."

She tries to introduce her students to contemporary writers, too—those who write about modernity, recent events, and things young people can relate to.

"Before the war, I asked my senior students to read something by Serhiy Zhadan—and now, we are following him on Facebook as he reports on his experience defending Ukraine," the educator adds.

The teacher is referring to one of Ukraine's most famous writers, who is originally from Kharkiv and who joined the army to defend his home city. Zhadan was nominated for the Nobel Literature Prize a week ago—an award that no Ukrainian writer has received so far.

"So now, we discuss his works in class as literature and reality are so connected," Lyubov says.

The woman is a homeroom teacher in a large town school in the Lviv region. The school has more than a thousand students, and now, it is getting more as the internally displaced children are starting classes.

"I am very worried for all of them," the educator confesses, "I try to be as sensitive as ever to all students, but especially to the new ones."

"Young people adapt differently," she continues, "They don't experience war the same way as adults, and it is our job to make them forget about the fighting by making them imagine better things. I make students write poems now, do some free-writing exercises, and just talk and adjust classes a little bit so they feel more engaged."

All the teachers received training on how to deal with stress and how to help students suffering from it.

"I thought that after 35 years, I would be ready for everything," Lyubov reflects, "But I was wrong. So, I am happy I got some ideas from our school psychologist."

Now, the teacher shares more personal experiences with her students—she tells them stories of growing up in the USSR and how that reality is different from modern Ukraine. She says that the students often don't believe her.

"I gave my fifth graders an assignment: they had to write what democracy meant to them," the woman goes on, "It was very difficult for children, but they came up with creative compositions. And then I told them that I grew up in a country where we could not say anything bad about the leader and that we could not celebrate Christmas because it was forbidden."

"The kids didn't believe me," Lyubov smiles, "they said that their parents complain about politics all the time, and nobody can ban Christmas. So, the students got distracted a bit. They didn't think about war too much, but about how I was deceiving them!"

Lyubov's school is now offering more extracurricular activities and social gatherings. For example, last week students prepared a concert and a patriotic show where they read poems by famous Ukrainian writers.

"I also invented a game for my younger students: they have to write compositions based on funny memes and photos," she says, "I googled some cats, and we had a class like this."

"I know it does not fit our educational program, but it gave children a good laugh, and we all needed that," Lyubov concludes, "I try to keep the kids positive, so they have fun at school even during the war."

What It's Like to Volunteer in Ukraine Now

Civil Society and the People During Times of War

September 2022

"It is going to get worse. People used to have their safety nets, their savings, but these are running out quickly," says Dina Kazatsker.

Dina is a community lead at the "Monster Corporation", the biggest charity foundation in Odesa. Odesa is an important port city in Southern Ukraine with more than a million residents and which is constantly shelled from the Black Sea.

When the Russian invasion started, many Odesa residents were scared that their city would be the primary target. This is because of the strategic location close to Crimea and the role Odesa plays for the Ukrainian economy.

"The first month was dreadful with everything being locked down, and many people leaving," Dina recalls, "It felt like half of Odesa was gone, and we were constantly expecting a major attack from the sea."

However, as Russian plans stalled, life returned to Odesa.

"People saw that Russians were unable to take the city, so they started going back home," Dina says, "Businesses started to reopen, and you could sense some normalcy coming back, too."

But this meant more work for Dina and her team.

Her organization was founded in 2017 although its origins date back to 2014 when a group of volunteers started helping the Ukrainian military. In a year, the charity raises up to 10 million Euros which goes toward various social causes. For example, during the pandemic, they provided oxygen masks to more than five thousand people. The team has 11 employees alongside dozens of regular volunteers.

"Monster Corporation" used to help our military even before the full-scale invasion. We also provided respirators during the covid pandemic and supported a lot of elderly people in Odesa,"

Dina says, "Now, the amount of people who need some support is much greater."

Primarily, the needs of the military have increased dramatically—there is a constant necessity to fundraise for weapons, vehicles, tools, and protective gear in addition to medical equipment. The government cannot cover all these expenses because there are too many of them, Dina explains.

"We get written requests from different military units asking for all sorts of support," the woman continues. "We understand that the state cannot take care of everything, especially in times like this, so we try to do what we can."

There is another problem, however.

"Many people lost their jobs and sources of income. The ports don't work, logistical chains were broken, and businesses went bankrupt," Dina says, "So many locals are surviving on their last money."

The positive thing, as the woman notes, is that the number of volunteers has increased exponentially. People are joining her organization, as well as many others in Odesa, to provide all kinds of support.

"We've got more problems, but we also got more people willing to help," Dina smiles, "These volunteers will never become indifferent because their help means they care about their country and their neighbors."

The volunteer movement in Ukraine has been on the rise since the start of the full-scale Russian invasion. 38% of Ukrainians are active volunteers across different non-governmental organizations, social movements, and charities. For example, Ukrainians managed to raise around 16 million Euros for four Bayraktar drones for the Ukrainian army in less than three days, all thanks to a digital volunteer initiative collecting funds.

Volunteers normally fill in those gaps which are not addressed by the government; they work independently from the state. The volunteer movement has seen rapid development since 2014. At that time, Ukrainians started organizing in communities and volunteer groups to help Ukrainian soldiers who were sent to Donbas. While the Ukrainian army was extremely under-equipped at that time, the volunteers were providing crucial help for the new recruits by raising money and buying ammunition, uniforms, and other necessities.

Everyone Is Struggling

In Lviv, Western Ukraine, the situation is somewhat similar to Odesa. The city, which is conveniently located only one hour drive from the Polish border, is a major cultural and economic center of the country. Lviv was also a victim of Russia missiles: the Russians destroyed some infrastructure objects and civilian buildings, killing locals.

Lviv welcomed the biggest amount of internally displaced people. There are around 700,000 in the city, and after the start of the war, around 200,000 Ukrainians moved there. So now, there is a major housing crisis as the city officials and volunteers struggle to house all the new arrivals.

Not all IDPs can afford their stay in Lviv, even with financial aid from the state.

"We are trying to help those internally displaced, and we deliver food for them when we have enough to give," says Anna Didyk, a volunteer at "Tarilka."

Her organization is a Lviv-based food bank which distributes unsold food from supermarkets to those in need. Before the war, "Tarilka" used to get a few tons of food per month to give to the locals. In 2021, the organization grew to 50 regular volunteers, saved 13 thousand tons of products, and registered nearly 3,000 needy to give food to regularly. The same year, the organization opened its own store where people could come and get groceries for free. Due to war, there is less food, and more needy.

"Now, we work depending on the availability of food. When we get enough products, then we organize giveaways and invite around 30 people per day to our store," Anna says, "But when we don't have enough food to make a worthy grocery set, then we send the food we got to charities which are willing to accept any help from us."

These charities, as Anna explains, help young people and families with many children. In addition, "Tarilka" sends food that can be stored for longer periods of time to people on the frontline as well as the military. For that, they rely on partnerships with local NGOs and volunteers based in the hot spots. For instance, "Tarilka" managed to distribute almost 2 million breads and more than a million of canned goods in Eastern Ukraine.

The difficulty is logistics and the fact that Ukraine is now suffering from scarcity of everything. As production halted in many regions, and unemployment and poverty are on the rise, people have fewer means to sustain themselves.

According to the projections from Ukraine's Ministry of Finances, the Ukrainian economy is going to shrink twice in size in 2022 due to the Russian invasion. Many businesses are starting to cut down the salaries of their employees because of smaller sales and other difficulties. As Ukraine is unable to export its goods and supply its production needs due to the destruction of many cities, the economic crisis is likely to affect more and more Ukrainians.

On Crimeans in Ukraine

Displaced People from Crimea Have Twice Been Victims of Russian Occupation

September 2022

"I am hopeful, but I am also cynical," Nika half-smiled at me, "I don't know how you combine these two feelings, but that's how I am now."

Nika is not her real name. She prefers to stay anonymous due to her professional affiliation. Nika is a former journalist, and now she investigates and collects information on Russian crimes in Ukraine. She says she does not want her job to intervene with her personal story.

"My job has always kept me very busy. Even before February 24, there were many things to map and connect because Russian influence is so vast in Ukraine and Europe as a whole," the woman explained, "Now, it is just like Armageddon in all of the senses."

The Occupation of Crimea

Nika is thirty. She has long brown hair, delicate fingers, and a very specific accent in Ukrainian, the accent that many native Russian speakers have.

"Gosh, I have forgotten Russian already, but I still sound like a Russian in Ukrainian," she laughed.

Nika is from Crimea, a Southern Ukrainian peninsula that Russia occupied in 2014. Back then, Russian soldiers took control of all administrative buildings in the region. Later, Russians organized a so-called referendum on making Crimea part of Russia. Since then, the peninsula has been considered an occupied territory by Ukraine and the rest of the world, while Russia started issuing Russian passports to the locals. People who refused to get a Russian passport could not reside in Crimea.

"My parents got Russian passports because they could not leave," Nika explained, "It is mostly because of my grandparents because they don't want to go anywhere else. My brother and I had to leave."

Crimea is an ethnically diverse region. Its population consists of Russians, Ukrainians, and Crimean Tatars, with the majority speaking Russian as the common language. People also learned and spoke Ukrainian as well as Tatar before the occupation. Now, both languages are persecuted, and any support or affiliation with Ukraine can land you a prison sentence.

"The last time I was in Crimea, I ended up in the police station. I had a Ukrainian flag in my car, and that is considered a terrorist symbol by the Russians," Nika recalled, "They told me if they see the flag again, I will not get off with a mere warning."

Someone reported Nika for the flag, and that is how she was detained. While she was at the police station talking to the officers, someone also pierced all the tires in her car, and the police said that they could not check the cameras to see what happened. The car was in the police station parking lot.

"We were actually lucky nobody killed us," Nika reasoned, "This is how the justice system works in Crimea now. I could not stay there after that."

Since 2014, the occupied Crimean Peninsula has received a large influx of Russians, especially policemen, security forces, government officials, and soldiers who came there as the Russian state was tightening up surveillance and control over the region. Many units of the Russian army have been moved from mainland Russia to Crimea, and they were crucial in attacking Southern Ukraine in 2022.

The Russian authorities also persecute dissent. Russian authorities launched a crackdown on Crimean Tatar and Ukrainian activists, jailing many on fake charges for decades. About 140,000 Crimean residents have left the peninsula since 2014 and resettled in mainland Ukraine because of the persecution. Below is a picture of an old mosaic of Vladimir Lenin, where someone wrote "Glory to Ukraine" in Ukrainian. You can be jailed or fined for saying that in Crimea.

"I have not been home for a few years, and I don't think I will come back there as long as Russians are in control," Nika said.

She moved out in 2014, right after the annexation, and settled in Lviv, Western Ukraine, later moving to Kyiv, the capital. Together with her husband, the woman later purchased a house a 30-minute car ride North from Kyiv. Nika also got a job as a journalist and, later, as a human rights researcher. She is now collecting data on Russian crimes against humanity in Ukraine.

"It is hard. It hits so close because everything literally happened at home," Nika said, her voice stern, "My new home."

The Occupation of Kyiv

"Russians stole everything. They took everything they could take from our home," she continued.

The Russian army occupied the areas North of Kyiv in early March, two weeks after the start of the full-scale invasion into Ukraine. The Ukrainian forces liberated the region in early April when the Russians retreated.

"I heard explosions on February 24, when the new invasion started," Nika said, "I was still in my house as I was planning to get ready for work. I used to drive to Kyiv a few times per week back then, but on that day, I was unsure where to go or what to do."

Nika's husband suggested that they stay home on February 24, and then follow the unfolding to decide how to act.

"In our garage, we had three cars. My husband used to be a trader; he was selling used cars as well as doing a lot of online trading before the war, so our home was always kind of like a storage space," Nika explained. The husband would buy the cars abroad and resell them in Ukraine, so there were always new vehicles around.

During the first three days of the full-scale invasion, the couple stayed where they were, but soon they decided it was too dangerous.

"We gave one of our cars to the local territorial defense forces. We used the other car to flee," Nika said. The third vehicle remained in the garage — the couple hoped to get it back when they would return home.

They packed the car with Nika's pet chinchilla, a pet cage, food, some clothes, snacks, and documents.

"We picked up my husband's parents, who also lived on the outskirts of Kyiv, and we drove to Western Ukraine," Nika recalled, "It was a freakishly long car ride, and it took us almost three days, but it was worth it. We would all be dead if we didn't leave."

Her face grew solemn as she finished saying this, and she showed me photos of her second home after the Russian occupation: everything was destroyed, there were cars and rubble on the streets and houses without roofs. Her voice, usually robust and strong, grew suddenly low and quiet.

"My neighbor was killed," she finally said, "His body was torn into pieces by homeless dogs because it was lying on the streets for a week. They only found a carcass."

A Broken Home

Nika's neighbor lived next door, his house is now nearly destroyed. Nika learned about his death in May when she visited her home for the first time after the Russians left the area.

"I remember driving back there and seeing what I saw, and I was getting emotional. All this time, I tried to keep my distance and stay as calm as possible, and I block all emotions, good and bad, but back then, I just could not," the woman recounted.

She saw the destruction of the region that had welcomed her and became her second home in 2014.

"Our house is one of the few that survived on the street," Nika said, "Russians took everything valuable and even things which didn't make any sense. The third car we left was gone, the TV, the washing machine, all the electronics, they even took clothes and some trinkets."

"My husband says that we now have to start from scratch because we're basically at a square one. But we're much better off than most of our neighbors because, at least, we still have a house," Nika sighed.

"I was unsure if I wanted to come back at first after all that had happened," the woman reflected, "Every street has seen so many deaths, there were corpses everywhere. I was worried about how to live with all this trauma and pain because it will definitely stay with people in the long run."

"But I decided that as long as Ukraine is here, I am here," Nika continued, "My husband agrees. We will restore our home and our country."

Now, Nika is collecting evidence of the Russian war crimes in Ukraine. She is interviewing people and helping preserve the testimonies of survivors. She is also working on identifying the names of the Russian soldiers who are accused of committing those crimes.

"It is a terrible task to hear and think of those crimes again and again when talking to people. I cry, and people cry as we recollect those stories and those memories," Nika says, "But it has to be done."

"I just think what will happen after the war. For now, people are still holding on because they have to; they don't have the luxury to break down and cry and just do nothing," the woman said, "But we are talking about a 40-million nation where nearly everyone is traumatized, and where we are facing about a huge collective pain that will take decades to address."

"I share this pain, and I fear for my people. It is so unjust what is happening to us, so inhumane," she sighed.

"But like everyone else, I pile up my emotions somewhere far so I can work, and I hope that I will have the strength to address these feelings sooner or later," Nika concluded.

I ask her if she believes Crimea will be liberated.

"Soon," she says, "I believe in the army."

Every Evil Has a Face

A Story behind Documenting Russian Crimes in Ukraine

September 2022

"Talking to the victims is the hardest part of the job," says Yanina Korniyenko, an investigative journalist from Kyiv. She works for Slidstvo.info, one of the most important investigative media in the country, with whom she has uncovered corruption and mafia schemes.

Now, Yanina focuses on documenting war crimes committed by the Russian army. Alongside her team, she is collecting testimonials and other evidence and collaborates with prosecutors who are doing similar work.

"The amount of war crimes that are being committed is overwhelming," the journalist says, "We hope that sooner than later our work will be used in the courts to help punish the guilty."

"We Have a Concrete Crime and a Concrete Perpetrator"

"Before the war, our job was completely focused on investigating corruption, law enforcement violations, and some criminal cases," Yanina explains, "But when the invasion happened, we had to change the work completely because we got completely different conditions and realities."

Her face is serious, solemn even. Her usually positive demeanor is different now, too: she is more restrained, more distant. I met Yanina six years ago when we were both trying out big media collaborations. Back then, Yanina struck me as someone who had the friendliest, the most optimistic attitude I have ever encountered. That is not necessarily how you would imagine an investigative journalist dealing with crime daily.

But Yanina defies stereotypes. In her mid-twenties, with long blond hair and big blue eyes, she has a natural capacity to make people like her and trust her. She listens well, and she makes people talk: two crucial things for an investigative journalist. Born and raised in Kyiv, she gathered a large pool of contacts across Ukraine, tapping into them for timely investigations.

Before the full-scale invasion, Yanina and her team underwent some in-depth training in OSINT or open-source investigations. The newsroom was expecting some military action from Russia, although it did not predict how big it would be. The team was trained on how to provide first aid, protect themselves, and understand how different arms were. This helped a bit during the chaos of the first days of the invasion.

"On February 24, we all woke up with explosions in Kyiv," Yanina proceeds, "We had a morning call with the team and decided to do what we could as fast as possible. We were the first newsroom that started looking for identities of Russian soldiers in Ukraine."

Their decision was intuitive. The team simply decided to use their OSINT skills and collect data on the troops invading Ukraine. The newsroom split; some remained in Kyiv, and others left for safer areas in Ukraine and abroad. Those in Kyiv managed to travel to northern Ukraine, which was liberated in April; they collected evidence and testimonies of victims. The rest worked remotely, verifying data and connecting with victims online.

Yanina was one of the journalists who left Kyiv. It was a personal decision, driven by her desire to protect her family, especially her elderly grandparents. She returned to Kyiv in May and does not plan to leave again.

"Through Testimonies from Mariupol, I Showed That It Was a Forced Deportation"

"We work on documenting all possible military crimes taking place in Ukraine and the consequences of Russian attacks, we talk to victims, and we identify the enemy," Yanina explains, "We believe that every evil has a face, and in this case, it is a face of concrete

Russian soldiers who came to kill Ukrainian citizens. That is why if we have an opportunity to identify them, we do it."

The team focuses on a locality that suffered under Russian occupation and tries to discover what Russian unit was stationed there, sometimes thanks to the lists from the Ukrainian law enforcement agencies. Then, using OSINT and social media, the newsroom looks for each soldier. With their photos in hand, journalists travel back to localities and ask victims to recognize the soldiers.

"This is how we develop a story," Yanina explains, "We have a concrete crime, and we have a concrete perpetrator of this crime."

"Another side of the work is to study what is happening in the occupied territories such as forced deportations and kidnappings of civil activists and journalists," Yanina says, "We talk to people who managed to flee or who are in contact with someone still there. This way, we try to identify conditions, specific locations, and potential legal documents which accompany forced deportation, such as migration cards. We try to collect as much evidence that a crime was committed, and that deportations were taking place against people's will."

Yanina started this work as an evacuee in Western Ukraine where there were many displaced people from Mariupol. She met and talked to some families, who shared their experience of fleeing the now nearly wiped-out city. 90% of the buildings have been damaged or completely destroyed. According to the mayor of Mariupol, at least 20,000 residents were killed during the early months of war.

"People barely had a chance to escape as Russians were constantly shooting at the humanitarian corridor. Only few cars managed to survive out of a large column," Yanina recalls the story.

Locals told her that some Mariupol residents tried to flee the warzone through Russia. So, she started looking for them.

The quest turned out to be difficult. The problem was once people were in Russia, it was nearly impossible to reach them, and they had problems leaving the country. Yet Yanina found enough people who fled Mariupol, then Russia, and managed to escape to different European countries. Through her contacts in the EU, she reached out to Ukrainians who agreed to talk on record.

Then, she connected all the testimonies to get the bigger picture.

"People were repeating the same things, such as that Russians interrogated children, separated them from families, and made people sign different documents," Yanina says, "Russians also imprisoned people who did not pass this filtration. Locals could not leave the buildings in which they were based during filtration, and they could not leave the train by which they were deported to Russia. Based on that, we could confirm that it was not a salvation, but a deportation."

"We have indirect evidence of war crimes. We have photos of immigration cards and booklets given to people who arrived in Russia," Yanina continues, "For example, Russians want to bring more people to their Far East and Siberia, so they are giving leaflets promising free land to Ukrainians who go there. There are videos and photos of filtration camps where people are located."

"The number of testimonies is overwhelming," she adds, "You can keep on collecting them for years before you get through even half. It is naive to state that all these testimonies are false. But if we are talking about factual evidence, until the city is occupied, we have no access to surveillance cameras. This is the only piece that's missing because camera footage can show Russian soldiers dragging people out of basements. This final evidence would fill the chain of events."

"We Hope Our Work Will Be Used in Courts to Help Punish the Guilty"

Once people are deported, they are placed under surveillance. Yanina investigates that, too. She discovered that the Russian Orthodox Church was responsible for many of the forcefully deported Ukrainians in Russia.

"When it comes to the Russian Orthodox Church, it does not hide its involvement in the deportations," the journalist says, "They advertise their services online and brag that they found shelter for many people. Shortly, the story is such: the Russian Ministry of the Interior is sending weekly announcements to the Russian Orthodox

Church with a number of adults and children who were deported to Russia. The Ministry also provides information on where Ukrainians should be directed. We got evidence that the Russian Orthodox Church is the one relocating the deportees across different monasteries. This shows that Church is collaborating with the occupiers."

"There is also evidence that the Russian Orthodox Church installed surveillance cameras to monitor Ukrainians: we have letters between church leaders that prove it," Yanina continues, "I wrote to the church myself to verify it, and they confirmed! They responded that it was true and that the Russian Orthodox Church finds nothing wrong with this activity."

Yanina hopes that this and many other discoveries will be used later in the international and domestic courts to bring the responsible to justice.

"We are already cooperating with Ukrainian prosecutors investigating war crimes in the Kyiv region," she says, "Journalists are invited to describe how they obtain certain information and share evidence that is used for criminal investigation. Our newsroom also trained prosecutors on how to identify Russian soldiers. We understand that law enforcement agencies are not always our close friends; very often, they are our opponents, but when we have a common enemy, we find ways to cooperate."

Yanina, however, has many concerns over how international law works and whether it can punish the guilty.

Western colleagues such as journalists and NGOs could help facilitate that process by shedding more light on the atrocities, but sometimes, their work is shallow and lacks background information.

"It is good that Western media report on Ukraine to the world, but given that the reporters do not have a lot of experience here and lack contextual knowledge, they cannot analyze the situation in a very profound way," Yanina explains, "They make overview pieces, but when it comes to documenting war crimes, only a few exceptional investigations touch upon these issues."

She provides an example of a recent story in The New York Times, which quoted Igor Girkin, a Russian veteran who played a crucial part in illegally annexing Crimea and managing the war in

Donbas. When the Times quoted him, his title was "Critic of the Ukrainian government."

"The NYT did not mention that Girkin is accused of shooting down the Malaysian plane MH17 which killed 298 people in the summer of 2014," Yanina exclaims, "Local journalists do better, more profound research."

"Access to Information Will Not Change Russia"

Yanina is skeptical whether verified news will impact the domestic situation in Russia.

"Our platform has a big percentage of views from Russia, which is weird because our content is only in Ukrainian," she says, "We only translated a few stories at the beginning where we identified Russian soldiers. Most likely, the views are from their relatives who want to know the fate of their children. However, they do not care much about the rest of what is happening. Even when the Russian Internet was free, it did not help them understand that they were living in an authoritarian state with a mad dictator. I do not think it will work now either."

Yanina herself struggles with the number of personal stories and pain she collects as a journalist.

"It is difficult to talk to victims because of all the trauma that people went through," she says, "They experience all of this again when they talk to you, and the memories of deportations and other horrors come back to haunt them. These people expect the interviewer to answer some rhetorical questions, and it is very hard to distance oneself and not to feel for them."

"Many journalists do become activists, which is an organic process for an invaded country," she concludes, "Lots of my colleagues have relatives who were deported or killed, and media makers cannot distance themselves from it. It is part of the job."

Russia Is a Terrorist State

It's Monday Morning, and Ukraine Is on Fire. Russia Launched 84+ Missiles and Drones against Ukraine

October 2022

I don't know how you start your work week, but here's how mine went: I woke up to running for my life into the basement. My cat outran me. My father followed. We felt it. A very strong shake. It felt like an earthquake. Then, loud noises. Explosions. More shaking. More noises. More explosions.

We are okay now. It's been a few hours, and the initial fear has passed. My hands no longer tremble, and I am just angry.

"I understand now how these people on the front-line feel," my father says. He was my basement companion.

For a few hours, we didn't have electricity, heating, or Internet. Russians targeted our tiny village in Western Ukraine simply because they could. It's less than 1,000 residents, no military infrastructure, just cute little houses in a suburb to a town in Western Ukraine. We're less than a two-hour drive to the NATO border, and we get bombed like this.

Russians hit in a place that's a thirty-minute walk from my house.

Luckily, no victims. Just a major infrastructure damage to the electricity grid.

"We're lucky they used those better missiles on us," my father says, "If they used their cheaper ones, those could destroy anything. They cannot be controlled."

I wonder if many Europeans still remember how to wake up to bombs falling on them.

"I Am Full of Anger"

"I was running when I heard the missiles," says Viktoriia Bilyavska, a resident of Kyiv. She is a woman in her early thirties, and she works as a communication manager.

"I like to run very early, but I felt like being lazy today, so I postponed my run," she continues, "I heard a whistle when I was almost done with my run, and I realized that something really bad happened. It took me a few good seconds to understand that it was actually a missile attack on Kyiv."

Viktoriia was in the center of Ukraine's capital, Kyiv, on the morning of October 10, Monday, when Russia launched a massive missile attack on the entire country. The woman was close to Shevchenko park, one of the most popular city destinations, when she realized that the city was being bombed.

"I passed the park maybe five minutes before the strike," she says, "If I were there earlier or later, I'd be dead."

She remembers noise and vibrations in the air, but she has a hard time putting the rest of the things together.

"As soon as I understood what was going on, I ran into the closest subway station," the woman explains, "It was right next to me, so I managed to save myself. More missiles were launched into the place where I was."

Russian rockets destroyed important parts of Kyiv's historical center. They targeted Taras Shevchenko University, one of the most important educational institutions, destroyed the park nearby, damaged a tourist bridge, and hit residential buildings. At least ten people were killed. Sixty are wounded, but the numbers are likely to rise.

"It reminded me of the first days of the war," Viktoriia says, "But even then, when we were all anxious, there were not so many attacks. This time, Russians launched more missiles than ever before."

"I Have No Mercy for Them. I Want Them to Live What We Live"

Ruslan is a resident of Zaporizhzhia. He and his family did not want to move out when the full-scale invasion happened. Zaporizhzhia is thirty minutes away from the invading Russian army; it is in a close proximity to Zaporizhzhia nuclear plant, the largest one in Europe, and which has been under Russian occupation since March.

Zaporizhzhia is also being under constant shelling. There are regular missile attacks on residential buildings. On Sunday, Russian rockets killed 17 people who were sleeping peacefully in their apartments. 89 were wounded. Zaporizhzhia was also targeted on Monday as well as during all previous weeks. The missiles targeting residential areas became a regular thing.

"In my store, the windows were broken because a missile hit pretty close from where I work," Ruslan says. His connection is unstable because a lot of mobile networks are overloaded in Ukraine at the moment as people are trying to reach their relatives across the country.

"I tried to convince my wife and son to leave the city a few months ago because it was too dangerous, but they decided to stay," the man tells me, "My son is about to graduate high school, and my wife works in the library. They did not want to go anywhere."

Ruslan, too, did not want to leave his home city when the war started; and he decided to stay even when Russia started terrorizing Zaporizhzhia daily.

"It is quite ironic that only a week ago Putin announced that he annexed Zaporizhzhia and that it is part of Russia," Ruslan says, "And yet, they keep on bombing us every day. If they consider us Russia, why do they bomb us? A bunch of terrorists!"

"Russia is a terrorist state, and anyone who sees what we've seen here in Zaporizhzhia will tell you what I tell you," the man proceeds, "They are trying to scare us, terrify the people, and that's why they kill us and destroy what they can. They know they cannot win, so they want to kill as many Ukrainians as they can in the meantime."

"I have no mercy for them," he adds, "Russians enjoy killing Ukrainians. I used to have friends in Russia, and they have all been celebrating the genocide of Ukrainians. They like what their government is doing, and they celebrate the war."

Ruslan has been running a small dairy store, but he is unsure whether he can keep it open anymore. However, people like his place a lot, and he still has customers, so he wants to keep on working for them.

"There are missiles and blasts every day now," the man concludes, "I shake every time, and I get scared, but I also know that I have to keep on working for my people. I cannot just abandon my home like that. Nobody wants to be a refugee."

"The last time, I remember the blast when the windows in my office broke," he says, "I fell to the ground and prayed to live. If I didn't leave my city then, I don't think I ever will."

Ukraine's Zaporizhzhia:
A City under Constant Attacks

This Southern Center Is Only 30 miles Away from the Russian Army

November 2022

"The situation changes all the time," Anna sighs, "Sometimes, we get relatively calm days and even weeks, and sometimes, we get bombed non-stop."

Anna prefers that I don't use her last name. A young woman in her early thirties, she works as a project manager in Zaporizhzhia. Anna has a pleasant, friendly face and a melodic voice which has a calming effect: even when she talks about the horrors of the Russian invasion, I still feel like listening to her more.

Anna is from Zaporizhzhia, a city in Southern Ukraine that is less than one hour drive from the territory temporarily occupied by Russia. Russians are constantly shelling the region and terrorizing civilians. Throughout October, they have been launching regular attacks on Zaporizhzhia, killing at least 70 residents. The bombing and shelling have diminished somewhat in the last weeks, although Russians have restarted their attacks after they retreated from nearby Kherson.

"We had two weeks of very intensive attacks," Anna recalls, "Back then, we were shelled morning, day, and night. With so many victims and wounded, it was a very difficult period. It was very hard for me."

Zaporizhzhia is home to nearly 800 thousand residents. However, when Russia launched its full-scale invasion of Ukraine, a quarter of the population left the city for other parts of Ukraine or went abroad. Another quarter moved to nearby villages and suburbs, hoping that shelling would be less frequent there.

At the same time, Zaporizhzhia received an influx of internally displaced people, too; the city is hosting Ukrainians who managed to flee Russian-controlled territories and are seeking refuge close to home.

"I Cannot Mentally Leave"

"We have heating, at least for now," Anna tells me, "So if Russians don't damage the critical infrastructure, we will have it in winter, too."

A lack of heating and electricity is not uncommon after Russia destroyed nearly 40% of Ukraine's infrastructure.

"The situation is a bit better now than before, but we can never predict how long this will last," Anna proceeds, "When there were fewer attacks, I managed to sleep at night during the entire week. This is a big deal for me."

When Russia was targeting Zaporizhzhia day and night in October, Anna could not sleep or work. She had to put her life on hold.

"At that time, it was very difficult to remain in the city," the woman says, "During that intensive shooting period, lots of people left. Many of my friends went away. Some left for a short time because it was impossible to sleep. However, many people stayed as lots of locals have jobs here and are linked to the city. I have many friends who work here and stayed throughout everything."

For Anna, constant October attacks were the worst.

"For me, it did not feel like weeks. It felt longer," she recalls.

During that time, there were lots of attacks on the right bank of the city. Zaporizhzhia stands on the Dnipro river, which separates the city into the left and right banks.

"The right bank used to be somewhat calmer before," Anna explains, "But in October, Russians attacked it more, so my perspective on the city and security changed. It was extremely difficult, both physically and mentally, for me. I could not work, and I could not sleep as many attacks took place at night."

"I think I became traumatized during that period which kept me tense all the time," she continues, "I left the city for a few days and went to Dnipro [a nearby city in South-East – Anna Romandash]. I needed a change. While in Dnipro, I could compare and reflect, and I saw that the situation in my home city was very tense."

Despite that, Anna returned a few days later.

"I was thinking about leaving Zaporizhzhia when we had those very intense shootings," she says, "Especially because there were so many attacks on residential buildings. However, I decided to stay because my husband is at the front line. This prevents me from traveling anywhere further than Kyiv. At first, I considered going to the capital, but it was not that safe at that time anyways. For now, I am staying home, and I will see what happens later."

"Local Government Lives in Its Own Reality"

Even under these conditions, the city keeps on living.

"I see lots of people in the parks, and it feels like there are enough residents anywhere you go," Anna proceeds, "Many people remain, especially volunteers who never left and keep on working and helping. Because the city is so close to the front line, volunteers have to be very dynamic to carry on despite everything. Some institutions are open, and some are closed. The city lives its life."

Residents are more cautious about their safety now.

"The streets make you feel more tense when there is an air alert," Anna explains, "In my case, I am more likely to seek shelter than a month ago, especially when I am outside."

She is unhappy with the local authorities and how they manage the war situation. For example, in Zaporizhzhia, basements are open only during the air alerts which warn the residents about an upcoming Russian bombing. However, there were many occasions when the city was targeted and shelled even before the sirens turned on.

"Zaporizhzhia does not have a lot of well-equipped shelters, and it is difficult for a lot of people working nights to be safe under these conditions," Anna says, "The local government did not provide a solution or show any empathy when dealing with this issue. It feels like the officials are either very incompetent or are ignoring the problems which matter for the city."

In addition, the local government received a lot of criticism from the civil society because of the poor handling of the humanitarian aid for the residents.

"There were investigations looking into the transparency of the process, but the results have not yet been shared with the public," Anna explains, "However, from what I see, most investigated people are still holding their official posts. This upsets me a lot, and it looks bad."

"I feel like the government is living in its own parallel reality," she adds, "For example, there is another case with Yalansky park in the city. A former politician from a pro-Russian party has been suing to get a permit to construct a mall there. The case was frozen for a long time, and recently, the guy won and got a permit from the city administration for the construction. This is a huge slap for the local authorities who allowed this. Locals are very disappointed and feel like the city government lives a life that is outside the real world."

However, the state government is opening some investigations related to the city and its key figures. In late October, Ukraine's intelligence services arrested former lawmaker Viacheslav Bohuslayev. The man is an honorary president of "Motor Sich", a Ukrainian aircraft engine manufacturer based in Zaporizhzhia. The company produces airplanes and helicopter engines; it is a strategic military enterprise.

Bohuslayev is accused of collaborating and assisting Russia and potentially providing the aggressor state with parts for its helicopters. In addition, he has Russian citizenship, which he hid as well as property in Moscow.

"This makes me happy to see that people like Bohuslayev are finally being investigated," Anna concludes.

Survivors Speak after Russia's Occupation of Kherson

People Have Been Tortured and Killed by Russians during the Kherson Occupation

November 2022

It has been three weeks since Kherson's liberation. Kherson is Ukraine's only regional capital that Russia managed to occupy since the start of its full-scale invasion. Russia also annexed the city and the region during its illegal referendum this year. On Nov. 11, 2022, the Ukrainian army entered the city as Russians fled.

Before leaving, Russian soldiers destroyed all critical infrastructure. The city that had almost 300,000 residents before the invasion has been without electricity, water, and heating. Ukrainian authorities are working to restore services, but this is difficult as the city — and the rest of Ukraine — are under constant bombardment by Russian missiles.

When Ukrainian forces freed Kherson, they discovered mass graves with the corpses of more than 400 civilians. They also found nine torture chambers. Locals recount experiences of persecution, threats, violence, and looting at the hands of the Russian forces.

Anzela Slobodyan is a former journalist from Kherson. She was at home when the Russian invasion started, and when Russian soldiers occupied her hometown. During the occupation, she was imprisoned for one month by Russian invaders and agreed to share her testimony.

"Not Everyone Survived"

"We were five women in one cell for three people," Anzela recalled, "We called our cell Ward No. 6." The moniker is a reference to a short story by Anton Chekhov, where he describes a mental institution. For Anzela, her imprisonment reminded her of that. She spent a month in the city's temporary detention facility, which Russians turned into a large torture chamber.

Anzela was taken to prison from her own house. Russian soldiers appeared on the doorstep of her Kherson apartment, put a bag on her head, and absconded her. Her partner Oleksandr was also detained although she was not informed about his whereabouts.

"Russians did not beat us," she continued, "They had other punishments for us. They were humiliating us, torturing us mentally, without any pity."

Anzela and her cellmates regularly heard other prisoners, men, being tortured in the cell next to them. Many were former soldiers or volunteers, some were regular citizens who dared to protest against Russian occupation, and others were just random locals. Anzela recalled listening to Russian guards arguing how to dispose of the body of a man they had murdered. She also heard a person raped in the neighboring cell. The noise of guards dragging a corpse through the hallway became a familiar sound.

"We knew it was our boys that were tortured with electrocution; they were beaten and forced to speak," Anzela said, "Russians did not know anything about the pain. They spread their toxicity into all living things. Wretched creatures."

"It was a terrible experience," she continued, "Every day we, the patients of Ward No. 6, began with the thought that we must survive. But not everyone survived."

Anzela's cellmate, a 66-year-old woman, had a heart attack while in prison and died. She was captured because her son was a local volunteer.

"My other cellmate was imprisoned because of her husband," Anzela proceeded, "And they released her when they no longer needed her. They took her for questioning and then told her: 'Your husband is killed, so you can go now.' That's one more lost life."

"Another cellmate was a teacher," the woman continued, "She was imprisoned because of her brother. She spent 33 days captive, without any questioning."

"I Hope to Forget Everything"

Anzela got her freedom after 30 days in captivity.

"On the next day after my release, I was already back at the prison," she recalled, "But this time, I was on the other side. I was waiting by the gates to bring some food for my former cellmate. She was there for four months for fake accusations."

All the women were released before the liberation, so they were able to celebrate the Russian retreat. However, Anzela is not celebrating yet.

"I know that 36 people were taken when Russians retreated," she said, "There were three women whose names I know, and I hope they will be discovered. When Russians release you from captivity, they take away your documents, money, and phones."

One of the captives is Kherson's mayor, Ihor Kolykhayev. He has been in captivity since the occupation. Despite many appeals from the local and international community to release him, Russians refused. Kolykhayev has serious health problems. When the Russians retreated, they took him with them. Currently, he is in Chaplynka, in the Kherson region, which is the part of the region that Russians still control.

Kherson is constantly being bombed from the nearby occupied area. There is a looming humanitarian crisis in the city as there is no heating while the temperatures fall below zero Celsius. However, locals remain resilient. Ukrainian supermarkets, postal offices, and trains are returning to the city; those who fled during the invasion are also slowly coming back.

This is also true of Anzela. The woman had trouble sleeping – while she was imprisoned Russians left the light on continually in their cell. She is also still trying to get rid of her traumatic memories.

"I hope to forget everything that I experienced," she concluded, "And to celebrate our victory with my former cellmates."

At least 200 people remain missing after Kherson's liberation.

What's Human about War?

A Question One Can Ask Every Day

December 2022

The answer comes uneasily during visits with Ukrainian women whose homes and loved ones are webbed into violence, pain, and fortitude.

"I don't know," Valeriia sighs. "It's a tough question."

We're sitting in a poorly lit kitchen as the sun says its final goodbyes for the day. Shadows grow longer as twilight sets in. I don't think Valeriia notices that. She is still somewhere else, in her thoughts, trying to answer her own question.

"I genuinely wonder every day, you know," she continues, looking at me. "What is it that makes you human? Is it enough to be born one to remain human throughout your life? That can't be it."

It's July, so it is very warm, despite the late hour. I get up to make another cup of tea for both of us as Valeriia answers a phone call. It is her husband.

"He's OK, but they had a few missiles coming in the central area," Valeriia says melancholically. "He told me his colleague got killed."

We don't speak for a while. The kettle alone disturbs the silence. I am not sure whether to stay or go.

"You're really too kind," Valeriia suddenly says. "It is so sweet to check on me. With all that's going on, I am sure there are lots of people who need help more than I do. And I do owe you my story, but I am just not sure it is any different from anybody else's. I left, but my husband stayed. I hope he comes here, but I cannot be sure. He is stubborn, and I love him for it. But my kids are here now, and this is where I will be.

"But mentally, I am still there." Her voice dies down.

Valeriia is from Mykolaiv in Southern Ukraine. She is in her mid-50s, and she used to work as an accountant in a bank while her husband taught physics in high school. When Russia launched its full-scale invasion of Ukraine on February 24, 2022, Valeriia was in her cozy Mykolaiv apartment. She had just woken up, and she knew something terrible had happened.

Mykolaiv is only 30 minutes away from the territories Russia has occupied since last spring. As heavy fighting continues in the area, the city is constantly under threat. Russian missiles target everything from pharmacies to kindergartens. The city didn't have running water for months, and it will not have heat during the long Ukrainian winter.

Valeriia decided to leave Mykolaiv in March. It was getting unbearable with all the shelling. Her husband, Viktor, decided to stay.

"I think it's kind of funny that he is the one staying behind and not me," Valeriia says, a sad smile on her face. "I mean, I am the one from Mykolaiv, and he moved there because of me."

Viktor is from Western Ukraine, a region farther from the front that is considered somewhat safer than the lands along the Russian border. Together with their daughter, son-in-law, and grandson, Valeriia fled west and found shelter in a small town near Lviv. They are staying in the apartment of a woman who is abroad.

"What is it that makes me a human?" Valeriia asks again. "What is it that makes others human? I have been helped tremendously by others, people I never met, people who welcomed us, people who gave us clothes and shelter — all while my husband is being shelled every day. He is being shelled by humans, too! Why do they do it?

"So, there must be something else that makes you a human, you see," she adds. "It is not enough to be born human. You have to act human, too. You have to make choices. Evil erases that humanity in you."

Borrowed Lives

My grandmother used to tell me, "Our life is a borrowed one. We never know when we have to give it back."

Isn't it so scary: the idea that we have no control over our lives because we never know when they might end?

Now the fear is getting more real. With every Russian missile, more Ukrainians die, and more Ukrainians will die. The realization that someone out there is trying to kill you is quite chilling. They are trying to kill you for who you are, and that makes it worse.

As I collect stories from people affected by the Russian war, they often share things they had not planned to say.

Olena, a 41-year-old woman whom my family hosted in our apartment, was reserved when we first met. She came to our little town with her husband, a son, and three grandparents. Her parents live in Kherson, a city Russia occupied for eight months. Unable to leave, they remain there today.

"My dad cannot move," Olena says. "He has been paralyzed since he had a stroke a few years ago. My mom was taking care of him, and so was my brother, but then the war broke out."

Olena's brother fled to Kyiv, where she used to live. He stays in the apartment she abandoned.

"We would have never left the capital if it wasn't for our son," she tells me. "He is in preschool and does not understand much of what's going on. I don't want him to spend his childhood in the bomb shelter."

Olena's older daughter is already married. She went to Belgium to give birth because she was pregnant when the invasion started. Olena does not mention this around her husband.

"I am so torn," she tells me, tears in her eyes. "I know she is an adult, but she is my child. And yet, I have another child here, and I have to take care of him. And my husband is counting the comrades he lost. What can I say to him?"

Olena's husband, Sasha, is a retired pilot. He was not drafted when the invasion started as he stopped flying military jets years ago. Many of his friends are in the army, and many have been killed recently.

"We don't talk much about it," Olena says, "He's gotten really quiet, and I don't know if it's good or bad to try to make him talk. He is very angry at Russia, and he is very angry at himself because he retired. But he knows they've got the best men there."

Women of Ukraine

Olena is unemployed. She worked as a secretary before the invasion. The small company that employed her went bankrupt.

"I didn't go to the unemployment office yet," she says. "I could not bring myself to it. I didn't particularly like my job, but now I miss it like crazy. I miss everything about my old life. My apartment in Kyiv, our loud neighbor whose piano used to annoy me so much, and constant traffic. I don't think we will go back to any of it soon."

This is maybe our third or fourth conversation. I suddenly realize that Olena has aged; she looks much older now than before, much older than a photo of her on social media. Her voice is getting more tired every time I visit her.

"I am very grateful to your parents for hosting us, but you have no idea what it's like to share a two-bedroom with your in-laws," she tries to joke. "I cannot wait to go home."

Olena's relatives sit quietly in another room. There is tension in the air as different generations try to comprehend what is happening to them. Sasha is outside with their son, Il'ko.

"Il'ko likes it here very much," Olena says, "He does not mind staying here for good, really. I wish I was more like him."

She shakes her head in disbelief.

"I was not prepared for this," she says.

At Least I Didn't Cry

Nadia was not prepared for the big war, either. But she knew something was coming.

"They never let us live," she says. "The Russians want us all dead."

Nadia is a businesswoman. She owns a clothing store that she runs by herself. She is also a fighter and a volunteer. In her late 50s, she has found her calling in community work.

"I don't want any of that aid we receive to get stolen, you see," Nadia says. "When there are resources, there are always people who want to take advantage of everything. So, we need good people to make sure bad people don't do anything shady."

Nadia started volunteering eight years ago when Russia invaded Ukraine for the first time, occupying parts of Eastern Ukraine and illegally annexing the Crimean Peninsula. Her husband became a soldier then, too.

"Yura volunteered right away," she says, pride in her voice.

Yura is almost 60 — a bit older than the average soldier. In his quiet Western Ukraine town, he worked as a gym teacher.

He was always in great shape, Nadia continues. "That's why they took him. You know, there were lots of volunteers, and all of them wanted to serve, but they turned down so many men. But they kept Yura because they knew how good of a soldier he'd be. And they were right."

Yura served for seven years in Eastern Ukraine and became the head of his unit. In 2021, he returned to civilian life. The family planned to build a house and move out of their Soviet-era apartment.

"Somehow, I knew it would not last." Nadia looks pensive as she speaks. We're sitting by the entrance of her store located in the town market of Novyi Rozdil, near Lviv. The place is normally busy, but it's been less crowded since the full-scale invasion. People shop less.

It is a warm and stuffy day, and it's hard to breathe under the Ukrainian sun in July. Nadia does not seem to mind. She is wearing jeans and a black T-shirt, and she's playing with her cat, which lives in the store.

"Yura was not happy when he came back from the east," she reflects. "He was angry more often, would get annoyed with small things, and always talked with his comrades on the phone. I knew he wanted to go to the front again. So, when the big war started, he was ready right away.

"We got into a big fight," Nadia says. "I told him to wait because I was so scared for him. Nastia started crying and begging him to stay. Well, I didn't cry. I knew better."

Nastia is the couple's daughter. Like her mother, she is a community activist working for the city.

"So, you see, my husband left angry," Nadia adds. "And I have not seen him since that day."

Nadia's son, Mykola, asked to join the army, too. He works in the local police force as an investigator. His bosses told him no.

"Thank God." Nadia manages a smile. "I would have lost my mind if he went. But we need cops here, too. We cannot just all go to the front line; we have to stay here and work."

Together with other local volunteers, Nadia is raising funds to buy gear and drones for the army. She helps sort the aid for internally displaced people and works to get them housed.

"We're a community of maybe 30,000 people," she says. "And we received around 2,000 in a matter of weeks. Where do we put them? How can we help?"

Nastia coordinates volunteers and public officials to address the influx of people, but the town simply does not have enough room. The displaced must sleep in gyms and college dormitories. Nadia encourages residents to bring blankets and clothing for new arrivals.

"God, I hate Russia so much," she says. "I hate everything they do. Just a week ago, I assisted at a funeral. Just a kid, 21, younger than my son. Killed in action. Russians killed him! And he's the only child! Now what are his parents going to do? What is left for them?"

Nadia tells me the soldier's girlfriend got sick at the funeral, so she had to take care of her.

"I think of those guys all the time," Nadia says. "Everyone had a story to tell, everyone had someone they loved and someone who loved them. I think about these children who will never be loved and kissed and hugged by their parents because there are no more parents. Dead. Just like that. Just because they can. Russians have no soul. I hate them so much."

"I think hatred is what keeps me intact, you know." She gives me a weird look. "I am so angry, so I don't worry about my husband all the time. I am too busy working and doing things and having all this anger in me."

Nadia has no intention of leaving Ukraine—not even if Russia goes nuclear.

"I would rather die than flee," she says. "I need to be here. Not just for the people who are coming. I need to be here for myself. I will lose my meaning elsewhere."

She holds her phone tightly as she says this. Her husband, wearing his military uniform, is the wallpaper. Nadia shows me a few images he sent her.

"He was supposed to come home for rotation, but he is the head of the unit, so he let other guys rest," she says. "I had a feeling he would sacrifice his time like that. He cares about others too much."

She smiles.

"You know, we don't communicate much because of security and connection and all," she says. "But whenever we communicate, it's like when we just started dating. It reminds me why I married him. I cherish every moment we talk."

Talk Later. In the Shelter Now

"Are you OK? Are your parents safe?"

Yana texts me from Kyiv. She is sheltering in a subway station as Russia unleashes more missiles against Ukraine's capital, one of many attacks that target critical infrastructure across the country. As winter approaches and Ukraine gets colder, such attacks can be deadly. Without electricity, heating, and water, many Ukrainians may freeze.

"I had no internet for a few hours. Sorry, I am getting back to you so late." Another text from Yana. "We're fine. Lots of people here. I will text you when I am back home."

Yana is a journalist from Kyiv. She is also my friend. When the invasion started, she took her family from Kyiv to the relative safety of Western Ukraine, but they returned home in May. She says they could not live elsewhere.

"Kyiv is my home." That's Yana again.

She is collecting evidence of Russian soldiers perpetrating crimes in Ukraine and on people Russia deported from the occupied territories. She hopes to get more information about the children who were forcefully taken away from Russian-controlled areas and put up for adoption in Russia.

"I tried a few times to imagine what a Russian person thinks," Yana says.

We are having a phone conversation. It is the day of the strike in Kyiv, but it is relatively calm now as we talk. There is no air siren, meaning Russia is not launching missiles, so people don't have to go into the shelter. Yana's connection is unstable, probably because many people are trying to make calls at the same time. Kyiv, like the rest of Ukraine, experiences regular electricity outages because so much infrastructure has been damaged.

"I am trying to understand how a person can not only accept but glorify all of this," Yana says. "They know what they did, and they like it. They celebrate it. They cheer the destruction, torture, and death. They hate us simply for who we are."

Yana is referring to the warmongering in Russia as ordinary citizens praise the government for the war and the destruction of Ukraine. She monitors Russian social media for her work.

"The level of hatred there is something else," Yana says. "They fear the Ukrainian army, so they encourage their government to kill women and children. Thousands of likes for people who praise raping Ukrainians. I cannot believe I have to read this crap."

I asked Yana if she plans to leave Kyiv.

"Not again." I hear a smirk in her voice. "I learned my lesson. Getting my family out of there was a pain but being outside of the home was an even bigger pain. We'll just have to stick around. People in Kyiv are not giving up.

"You know, Ukrainians are probably the maddest people in the world," she says, with a hint of a smile. "We criticize our government, always find fault in everything, and can be such morons. But that's when things go well. When things go bad, when we're at war, we suddenly show our true colors. We're brave, and we're kind, and we're hopeful, and we're fighters. I have received more kindness and help in these months of war than during all the previous years of my life. I love my people."

Yana's voice starts to tremble. She tells me she has to go and she will call me later.

We text each other regularly—just to check on each other. Ukrainians now need to text their loved ones just to know if they are still alive.

I Believe in Ukraine

On October 10, Russia launched a missile attack against my home village of Hranky-Kuty, south of Lviv. A tiny place of fewer than 1,000 residents, it was hit by a few multimillion-dollar missiles that damaged the electric grid.

The attack felt like an earthquake. There was a whirring noise, and then the walls shook. And again.

People ran wherever they could. Most hid in their cellars. The connection was lost.

Hours later, when the electricity was restored, my father and my cat came to their senses.

"I did not expect we'd get attacked," my father says. "I mean, 15 million dollars to hit us? And we fixed the damage in less than a day!"

Not every locality is this lucky. Many are still without any electricity, many have no heat, and many lack water. People are buying blankets and wood to keep warm.

"It's going to be a very tough winter," my father says. "But we will manage."

"But for how long? How is this all going to end?" I ask.

"I don't have a timeline for you. But Russia cannot win. We cannot just disappear, Anna."

He looks at me intently.

"You see, the best of us dies. The best ones are being killed. It's very sad. It is a tragedy, Anna. I don't think about it often because it's enough to make a sane person go crazy. But they won't kill us all. They can't. Nothing can kill the idea whose time has come."

"Now you're just being dramatic."

"But that's true, kiddo," he sighs. "It looks very grim, I know, and it feels like the apocalypse, but we will live through it, and we will rebuild everything. We will rebuild better. I never felt more alive than now. Don't you?"

I nod.

"You see, all these people who are volunteering, who are fighting, who are helping. Why are they doing it? Why not fleeing? Why not surrendering? But that's who we are! We fight for what we love. It's the only thing that makes sense."

"And we love Ukraine," I say quietly.

"And we love Ukraine," my father agrees.

How Russia Stole Ukraine's Christmas

With Constant Bombing and Little Electricity, Upcoming Holidays Are Not So Cheery for Ukraine

December 2022

Ukrainians like to go big on Christmas; in fact, they like it so much that they celebrate it twice. The first official Christmas holiday is on December 25. The second one is January 7. Both celebrations are followed by the twelve traditional meals, caroling, and impressive Christmas markets.

This year, the celebrations will be very different. Due to the ongoing Russian invasion and constant bombings of civilian infrastructure, millions of Ukrainians are left without heating, water, and electricity. In addition, many are struggling financially as they lost their jobs and housing due to the Russian war.

Across Ukraine, people are slowly starting to prepare for the upcoming holidays. In Mykolaiv, a regional center in the South only thirty minutes away from Russia-occupied territories, the city authorities installed a Christmas tree decorated with camouflage nets and military-inspired ornaments. The tree is a reminder of the hardships soldiers and civilians all have to endure.

"It's tough times, so the holidays will reflect that," says Eugenia Hlushchenko, a Kharkiv resident. Kharkiv, Ukraine's second-largest city, is only one hour away from the current frontline in the East. The city is constantly under shelling from the Russian army; bombings and destruction of civilian buildings have become an ordinary occurrence.

"I remember that every year, there would be huge debates on Christmas decorations and how much we're going to spend on that from the city budget," Eugenia laughs, "It now feels like it was a different era; it's so surreal to think that we had such a good life and bothered ourselves with such things."

In Kharkiv, there won't be a big Christmas tree in the city main square as in normal times. Instead, the city authorities installed smaller Christmas trees in some bigger bomb shelters and metro stations where people go during air alerts.

"I thought it was a very smart effort, and it was nice to see those Christmas decorations at least somewhere," Eugenia reflects, "The city is mostly dark as we're saving electricity, so having Christmas lights is a luxury in this environment."

For Eugenia, she plans to stay at home for the holidays and spend more time with her family while decorating a little plastic tree and cooking kutya, a traditional Christmas dessert. She has a son of preschool age who does not go to kindergarten now because of the war, and her husband works in the bank in the city.

"We spend many nights in the corridor or go to the subway when there is an air alarm," Eugenia says, "When there is no heating or electricity, I go to subway or train stations to charge my phone and warm myself up. It is very difficult with a little kid."

For Christmas, Eugenia plans to cook traditional Ukrainian meals; this year, she will also celebrate on December 25 instead of January 7, when most Orthodox Christians observe Christmas.

"For Christmas, I wish for victory and a peaceful future for my child and all the children of Ukraine," she says.

"This Holiday Season, We're Celebrating Our Army"

Unlike Kharkiv, Kyiv will have a Christmas tree on the city's main square although it's going to be very different from last year. This year the tree will be smaller and with energy-saving lights. There won't be any Christmas markets or usual festivities on the main square.

"The weather is dreadful; everything is dull and cold," Yana Lyashuk says. A resident of Kyiv, she wants to travel to Western Ukraine for the holidays to spend time with her partner's family.

"My boyfriend is originally from the Donetsk region; his family home was destroyed," she says, "Now, his parents are sheltering near the Hungarian border. We stayed with them when the invasion started, but then returned to Kyiv in the summer. Now, we want to go back to see them."

Yana and her partner live in a very fortunate place in Kyiv; their apartment building is right next to the hospital, so they almost never get electricity cuts as they share the same electricity grid with the medical institution. They also have stable heating and water supply.

"Unless there is a major bombing, we have a connection and other utilities," Yana explains, "So sometimes, I work from home instead of going to the office because there we may not have any electricity."

Yana rarely goes to the city center now because of the bombing scare; the downtown area is more likely to be targeted, she believes. Yet, she wants to see the Christmas tree once it's installed.

"We will have a very modest celebration this year, and I think that's true for most Ukrainians," she says, "We're very grateful to be alive, and we will celebrate our army this season because we get to have the holidays only because of them. I won't be spending money on gifts; I'd rather donate to the Armed Forces."

"I also want to take a photo in front of the Christmas tree because with or without lights, Kyiv is so beautiful," Yana adds, "I know that this year's tree is called The Tree of Unbreakables, and I think it is a very fitting name."

Holidays Are Not as Cheerful This Year

"I kind of forgot that the holidays were coming," Maryana Oleksiv says. She is from Lviv, the biggest city in Western Ukraine, well-known for its Christmas market and festivities. Normally, Lviv has a big tree, hundreds of thousands of tourists, many carolers on the streets, and various shows and performances across the city.

This year, Lviv will have none of that. The city administration decided that there is no money or energy to spare for any celebrations. Lviv residents sometimes get electricity for only four hours a day, so the residents have to be very resourceful in order not to freeze this winter.

"I bought myself thermal underwear, and that's the gift I will get my relatives," Maryana says. Despite the need to work in nearby cafes which have generators, she is hopeful.

"I donated money and bought some thermal underwear for the soldiers, too," she adds, "And I am excited about the holidays, although, to be honest, the days are very blurry, so it's not like I am preparing for any special day or something."

"I spend part of my time at my boyfriend's and the other part at my mom's, so I commute between places whenever there is electricity," Maryana continues, "Given that I cannot work as much as before as my job requires steady Internet, that commute fills up the free hours I have."

Maryana's family is all in Lviv; they have prepped for the winter by getting many blankets and layering up. Maryana has not yet bought a generator, but she is considering it.

"My boyfriend suggested that if we keep on getting so many blackouts, we'd need to get some generators before the New Year," she says, "So maybe, that's going to be an investment we're going to make in 2023."

"I've never experienced anything like this winter," Maryana reflects, "And I never thought that my thirtieth Christmas will be during the war in my country."

"But it made me appreciate what I have more," she adds, "Many of my friends are in the trenches or have been wounded in battle, so I know it could be much worse."

Maryana traveled to Paris for work at the end of the fall, and she could not believe her eyes when she saw the abundance and the many lights in the French capital.

"Seeing how dark Lviv is and how we value electricity and simple things made me forget that very close to us, people lead a very different life," the woman reflects, "I didn't realize how quickly I adapted to the war reality and how this survival mode became the new normal for me."

"But I Go On"

In Ukraine, the People Fight to Repel an Invader, Resisting Not Only the Physical Devastation but the Emotional Paralysis that Threatens a Population under Siege

January 2023

It's January 1, New Year's Day. I went to bed around 11 p.m. on December 31 and did not wake up for the midnight countdown. I slept through an air alert and 45 missiles and drones that Russia launched against my country in the first hours of 2023. I learned about the attack only after waking up.

A day earlier, on December 31, we had an air alert for about four hours. Russians launched missiles and drones again, targeting anything they could target. In the past, they used to strike electricity grids and other critical infrastructure. Now, as Ukrainians learned how to counter missiles more or less effectively, Russians are attacking whatever they can in hopes of causing most destruction. At least two people were killed, and a few dozen are injured. That's how Ukraine enters 2023.

As I wake up to the new year, I read my friend's tweet.

"Department for infants of the Kherson Regional Children's Hospital. The hospital where my mother works. A few minutes before the New Year, Russians started shelling it. Nurses saved the children, no one was injured. Almost all other buildings are damaged. Russian army is sick."

The tweet includes four pictures of destruction. Rubble and trash in what used to be a hospital hours ago.

I look at the images, and I suddenly feel very tired. My husband calls it emotional paralysis.

I've learned to tune out a lot of things recently, such as the sound of the air alert, or the news or the occasional church bells

103

announcing the burial of another victim of Russian aggression. It is difficult to live in war.

Many Ukrainians are fighting against this emotional paralysis. They love, care and hurt, but they learned to doze their feelings and not let negative emotions consume them. They learned to manage hope and empathy, too, so these don't overwhelm them.

"People are getting more and more tired," Yana told me a few days after Christmas when she visited me in Lviv.

Yana is a journalist from Kyiv and a friend. We met in a big mall near my house, and she was very anxious when we went there. Yana hoped there wouldn't be a siren announcing an air alert so we wouldn't need to rush to evacuate ourselves. We were lucky. No sirens at that time.

As we sat in a cozy café inside the mall, we talked about life, death, war and other troubles.

"So many people are getting low on energy," Yana said. "It's like we're running a marathon, and it doesn't seem to end, and we have to keep running because the track behind us is on fire."

I feel her.

Yet Yana keeps working—just like millions of Ukrainians who, after 10 months of constant bombing, death, and destruction, learned how to survive and how to live.

And today is another day, and it is glorious. It is very warm for Ukraine, almost 60 degrees, and it is sunny and fresh. I'm not sure if this is the best weather for our troops in the south and the east, but at least they're not cold.

Ukraine Goes On

In the rear, we're not complaining either. Nadia is hopeful, despite her husband serving in the very hell of Bakhmut, a city Russians cannot conquer, so they vowed to destroy it. She bought two kilos of walnuts for the holidays and made the special dishes we cook for Christmas. She goes to work regularly, and she volunteers.

Her husband visited her a month ago. He finally got his leave for two weeks and stayed with her in the relative calm of Western Ukraine. Nadia still holds on to that time.

"He told me Bakhmut was a meat grinder," she said. "But he calls almost regularly, and that's enough for me."

She doesn't know when she'll see her husband again. He fought for almost eight months before he got his leave, and there's no way of knowing when another break will be.

"I worry about him," Nadia continued. "But I go on."

Life does not stop for Valeriia either. Originally from Mykolaiv in the south, she's now splitting time between her old home and the new one in Western Ukraine. After Kherson, a major Southern city, was liberated, she finally visited her husband, who stayed in Mykolaiv.

"I felt like I could go there now that our troops pushed Russians farther away," she told me. "We still get bombed regularly, but people are staying no matter what. So, I felt brave enough."

She stayed with her husband for two weeks and then came back to her kids and grandkids in the Lviv region.

"I know that, rationally speaking, Mykolaiv is extremely dangerous," she said. "But it was important for me to come home. I don't know how to describe that state, but it just felt very right and good. I know we'll win soon, and then, I won't need to choose between my husband or my safety."

It's true that even Western Ukraine is not safe; Lviv receives major attacks, as do other cities and villages across the region. People run to the shelters and sing songs, call their families, and even try to do work. It's impossible to schedule your life around bombing, electricity cuts, and other stresses, but Ukrainians are getting pretty good at it.

"We're going to have to do a ton of homework when the war is over."

That's my dad.

"We're actually already starting it," he continued. "We'll need to rebuild, better and more inclusive, and we'll need to take care of ourselves. We cannot lose our minds when we finally win."

I worry about that, too: about people's souls and how to save them so they don't carry all the trauma and damage after the war. I worry about Ukrainians, myself included, but I have no doubts about our resilience.

I am turning 30 in a few days, and while I don't celebrate my birthdays much, I will have a small celebration this year. I'll donate more to the army, and I'll meet with a friend I have not seen in a year. Maybe I'll go to the theatre, too, as I haven't been there in a long time. Those small things matter, and I, like millions of Ukrainians, appreciate them.

It's strange to live every day with a realization that someone out there is trying to kill you. That someone is a Russian soldier, a person out of flesh and blood, who hates me for being me. But I won't let that hatred break me. I have to live: work, dream, and build, so others can do the same.

As we're entering this year rather solemnly, with caution and restrained emotions, we remain hopeful. My mom told me that people were singing songs and shouting "Glory to Ukraine" throughout New Year's Eve. It happened all over the country. People filmed themselves singing in the basements as they were welcoming 2023.

I, too, am hopeful and grateful that I am alive and that I've got a big blue-and-yellow flag in front of my house. Before the big war, we'd put it there for Independence Day and other holidays. But last year, we've kept it since February 24.

It's still standing, and it will stand.

"Brave to Rebuild" in Ukraine

Young Ukrainians Volunteer to Restore What Russian Troops Have Destroyed

January 2023

"I remember my first-time volunteering," Zhenia told me, "We were driving toward our destination and being really loud on the bus. But the moment we entered Irpin, everyone got quiet. Through the windows, people stared at the ruins in front of them."

She sighed.

"It may sound strange and sad, but I am already used to seeing the destruction," the girl added, "It no longer provokes very strong emotions in me as it used to."

Zhenia Pohorila is a young adult, barely out of her teens. Originally from Kyiv, she has pink hair and a calm, comforting voice. Born and raised in independent Ukraine, she reminded me once again how Gen Z was making a difference in their home country.

Zhenia is a communication coordinator at Brave to Rebuild, a volunteer movement that grew from a dozen students into a mass organization that helps rebuild from the damage of the Russian occupation. I discovered Zhenia and her team by accident when I was looking for people regularly traveling to formerly occupied areas: Brave to Rebuild members were going every weekend and, sometimes, during the week too.

"The organization materialized in mid-May, although at first, nobody planned to turn it into anything formal," Zhenia said, "In the beginning, it was a meeting of eight people who were friends and acquaintances. They were mostly graduates from Kyiv Mohyla Academy and Ukraine's Leadership Academy."

The eight friends simply wanted to help. When they gathered for the first time, it was one month after the Kyiv region was liberated. Volunteers went to the city without any contacts; they saw a damaged building, entered, and started asking locals whether they

107

needed any help. After that, they decided to create a name, search for more volunteers, and expand.

In half a year, the team grew tremendously and now involves a few thousand volunteers who come whenever they want to help with cleaning the rubble and other activities. Most volunteering takes place in the Kyiv region, in the towns most damaged by Russians: Irpin, Borodyanka, Hostomel, and Bucha. The team plans to volunteer in other liberated areas and has already traveled to Kherson and Kharkiv regions, bringing humanitarian aid and generators there.

"Since mid-May, there wasn't a single weekend when we didn't volunteer," Zhenia said, "Despite the cold, people still come, and not only on weekends. In addition, we have lots of foreign volunteers. People normally hear about us through word of mouth from friends who are already with us. That's how I learned, too."

"90% of our work is cleaning the rubble," the girl continued. "Sometimes we help with construction when the owners already have some equipment, and we're there to aid them."

A few times, volunteers helped tear down entire houses or some walls or roofs. This activity is very popular, and people call it "anti-stress." However, the organization does not do a lot of construction work because the volunteers lack the skills for that. On a case-by-case basis, the team sometimes hires construction specialists they know to help locals.

"Our House Is Gone"

"When I arrive at these locations, I have to coordinate and organize volunteers, so I handle that quite unemotionally," Zhenia reflected. "The realization that we're cleaning what used to be someone's house comes only later."

"For me, the biggest trigger is seeing some nice tiles in what used to be someone's kitchen or bathroom," the volunteer continued. "That's when I realize that this is the place where people would stand barefoot and make breakfast for their family during the weekend...I tried to get rid of these thoughts right away because it makes the work much more difficult. For many volunteers, the trigger is seeing nice plates and kitchen utensils that survived intact."

According to Zhenia, volunteers often discover some things that survived the bombings while clearing the rubble in the house. For instance, once the team found some pretty glasses made out of crystal. The volunteers brought them to the homeowners, who were very careful and gentle with these things. They wanted to save them from any damage. However, there are also homeowners who don't feel the same attachment to their things anymore. Zhenia recalled a few locals telling her, "Destroy it and get rid of it. Our house is gone" whenever she'd bring them anything that was rescued from their former home. Homeowners are almost always there when volunteers arrive, and they work together to get rid of the rubble.

"Homeowners are very grateful," Zhenia said, "It is very difficult when they show us the pictures of what their house looked like before the Russian invasion because all we see now is rubble. People are very sweet; they often feed us when we're there. Volunteers joke that they want to go to the locations where homeowners feed them borsch."

"I remember one time, we volunteered in Irpin, and a woman whose apartment was destroyed worked with us non-stop," the girl added, "She said: 'If I cry, it won't help me. But if I help you, we can clean faster, and we can rebuild faster.'"

According to Zhenia, most locals she encountered were very optimistic, especially after seeing the number of volunteers who want to help perfect strangers, and said, "This inspires them even though they are already very strong." The girl added, "It is very sad to see what happened to these locals because they are very kind. I don't understand why they had to endure that injustice."

Residents often share stories about their destroyed houses. Some people finished reconstruction days before the invasion. Others stayed during the occupation even though their homes were destroyed because they were feeding dogs whose owners were killed.

"We get very affected when we see someone crying next to their house or telling us 'This was my son's room,'" Zhenia continued. "Right now, we are collecting money for a family that has a daughter who is two or three years old. Before the invasion, the family renewed the girl's room and bought her a new princess bed. The little girl was telling everyone: 'I used to have a princess bed, and I really liked it, but I don't have it anymore.' Of course, it is very difficult to hear that, but it motivates us to work better."

The team launches fundraisers to help local people and shares their stories. Everything the organization buys is either crowd-funded or given to them for free, and volunteers also organize charity events to raise funds for people they encounter through volunteering. Those who cannot donate money give their time.

"People can donate to us via PayPal or other means or join us as volunteers. It's the best help," Zhenia said.

"When people volunteer with us, they see their direct impact." The girl continued, "When they arrive on location, all they see is a mountain of rocks, and in a few hours, they have 100 bags of trash with rubble. They understand that they did that, and it makes them feel better. This shows that their donations and volunteering go somewhere useful, and they feel happier about it."

"Towns Are Coming Back to Life"

"Even though we clear the rubble inside the house, the damage is still there," Zhenia said. "You see it whenever you walk the streets."

However, locals are coming back in large numbers. Some are staying with their neighbors whose houses survived; others live in garages or commute daily from Kyiv. Cafeterias and public spaces are reopening too.

"People are covering the bullet holes in their houses because those were everywhere," the girl said. "It feels strange seeing children running around those destroyed streets and realizing how quickly we accepted this reality. But the towns are coming back to life."

For Zhenia and her team, the next step is to spread the work they are doing to other regions of Ukraine where help is most needed. They are currently figuring out the logistics of how to aid other liberated areas.

"We want to help more and more given that we already have this experience and a name that people recognize," she said, "We have a great potential to expand, and we want to help where we can help the most."

For the activist, this volunteering experience was an important personal and professional step. She was always interested in communications, but never worked in the field. This experience helped her learn how to launch successful campaigns from scratch and gain thousands of followers for a cause.

"I really like Brave to Rebuild because you can see the impact of your work every day," the activist said. "Whenever we update our monthly results, we see how much we did, and it is great that instead of waiting, we're doing something as we speak. Our work helps people now."

"Of course, I wish none of us had that experience, and that there was no war so we wouldn't need to rebuild any of these houses," the girl continued. "However, we have what we have, and I see a huge value in empowering so many people to volunteer even if they have never done that before."

Zhenia's team is also lobbying for a volunteering culture and hopes that people will stick to it and continue volunteering even after there are no more houses to restore or clean.

"I feel my impact because my job is to involve volunteers to provide more help." She concluded, "Whenever I volunteer and share this with my friends, it motivates others. Whenever my friends want to hang out with me, I'd always say: 'Let's meet during the weekend in Irpin.' Whenever you lead by example, people respond to it better."

A Family Struggles to Reunite under Russian Occupation

Six Siblings Spent Four Months Detained in Occupied Ukraine, Separated from Their Parents

February 2023

What started as an idyllic family visit to a health resort turned into a nightmarish separation when the Russian occupation of Ukraine disrupted the Lopatkina's family's annual health retreat. The six siblings ended up spending four months stranded and held by Russian forces before eventually joining their parents as refugees in France.

When Russia's full-scale invasion of Ukraine started on February 24, 2022, six of Olha's nine children were in Mariupol, in a health resort where they were getting their annual health check-ups. When the occupation began, Russian troops blocked the roads in and around the city, locking the children at the sanatorium and restricting the parents' access. The family was separated for four months.

"The Nurse Told Us That the War Started"

Olha's family is from Vuhledar, a mining city in the Donetsk region, some 50 miles away from Mariupol. Olha is a music teacher, and her husband Denys — like many local men — worked as a miner.

In 2016, the couple decided to adopt their first child. Then, the second. By 2018, they had already adopted seven children in addition to their two biological kids. The family moved into a townhouse given to them by the authorities and kept on living in their little town. Vuhledar is close to the so-called Donetsk and Luhansk People's Republics — Ukrainian territories occupied by Russian proxies since 2014. Despite that, the town remained calm all the way until 2022. As I am writing this, the area around Vuhledar is where some of the heaviest fighting is taking place.

114 WOMEN OF UKRAINE

However, back in January of 2022, few in Ukraine believed in the probability of a full-scale war with Russia. So, Olha sent six of her children to the resort in the nearby Mariupol. That was not their first trip there. Every year, the children would go there for a few weeks to improve their health. The resort had its own teachers so the kids would not miss classes, too.

A health resort is a common occurrence across Central and Eastern Europe. It is a mix of an all-inclusive hotel, a hospital, and a spa. The visitors stay in the hotel, which has its own medical staff. The doctors check all the visitors, prescribe any necessary medicines and medical procedures, and help them improve their health. Targeted toward improving wellness, the health resorts aren't necessarily linked to disease, families will go as a preventive measure, like the Lopatkinas who made it an annual ritual. In Ukraine, children from large families and other vulnerable groups can get free passes to stay there.

"I loved that resort so much," said Tymofiy, Olha's oldest son. Tymofiy is a senior in high school, and last year's trip to the resort was supposed to be his last. As he was about to turn eighteen, he would no longer be able to get a free visit to the resort.

As the eldest, Tymofiy kept an eye on his five younger siblings; the youngest was barely six. The children were planning to stay until early March. Two other children were with their parents in Vuhledar, and the oldest daughter was in Western Ukraine for a sports contest when the full-scale invasion started.

At 5 am on February 24, 2022, the nurse woke up the children. She gathered all residents in one room.

"The nurse told us that the war started," Tymofiy recalled, "She also told us to call our parents so they would take us home. I called mom immediately."

To get from Mariupol to Vuhledar, the children would have to pass through Volnovakha, a town that was already bombarded from the first day of the invasion. The family could not drive through there, so the parents told the children to wait for an official evacuation.

"During the first days, it was completely fine in Mariupol," Tymofiy said, "We played videogames, watched movies, relaxed. We still had Internet and electricity, so it was all right."

As the invasion continued, the resort became more and more empty as parents came to pick up their children. Tymofiy and his siblings, however, remained as their family could not get through the fighting. By March, the city of Mariupol was turning into a bloodbath as it became the epicenter of the heavy fighting. On March 1, Tymofiy managed to call his mom for the last time. By then, all the resort management had fled. The children remained with a few of the employees, and soon, more residents from Mariupol started coming to shelter there. The idyllic resort was turning into a refugee camp and bomb shelter.

"We had no heating and electricity," Tymofiy remembered, "It was me and a few other guys who would go around the territory, cut out some trees, and use the wood for fire. We'd get some water from the nearby Azov Sea and boil it. That's how we cooked, that's how we washed ourselves, and that's how we kept ourselves warm."

The resort was bombed, too, so the children and adults quickly had to move to the basements and only went out to cook food and gather wood.

Months Away from Parents

For Olha and the rest of her family, staying in Vuhledar was bad, too. Russians bombed the town already on February 24. Nearby towns were targeted as well.

"We were scared," Olha said, "We didn't know what to do. It was dangerous to go to Mariupol, so we were just agonizing and trying to decide. I was scared to go."

Olha reached out to the local authorities hoping they would evacuate the children. But they were unable to help.

"We called the children every day hoping that the heavy fighting would end soon," Olha continued. By March, the family had moved into the basement of their house and were hosting six more people who had fled nearby Volnovakha.

On March 6, the family decided to flee. They quickly packed and moved to Zaporizhzhia, a city in Southern Ukraine. The next day, they moved to Western Ukraine, where they picked up their daughter. And, a day after, the parents and three children crossed the Ukrainian border. In their white SUV, they traveled to France, where they settled as refugees.

Tymofiy and his siblings were still stuck in Mariupol. On March 18, the Russian authorities allowed a humanitarian corridor to evacuate civilians from Mariupol. A local volunteer came to pick up Tymofiy and his family. On that day, around 9,000 residents of Mariupol managed to flee to Ukraine-controlled territory. The Lopatkina kids, unfortunately, were not so lucky.

Russian soldiers recognized the local volunteer who was driving the children.

"The soldiers knew the driver was a pro-Ukrainian activist, so they did not let him drive us to safety," Tymofiy said. The soldiers took his car and made all the passengers leave. "Despite our protests, the soldiers took us, and on the next day, sent us to Donetsk."

Detained in Donetsk

Donetsk is the biggest city in Donbas, an industrial region in Eastern Ukraine, parts of which have been under Russian occupation since 2014. In Donetsk, Russian proxies established the so-called Donetsk People's Republic.

It was Eleonora Fedorenko, a spokesperson for children's rights in the so-called republic, who ordered children to be brought to Donetsk instead of going on to Ukraine-controlled territories.

"Eleonora would come to see us with journalists from Russia Today," Tymofiy said, "They would bring presents and record everything to show on Russian TV. They would never come without cameras."

Later, the recordings were used on Russian TV channels for propaganda purposes: children were shown as survivors rescued by Russian troops. The Russian journalists did not mention that the children were in Donetsk against their will.

"It was impossible to live there," Tymofiy said, of his time in Donetsk. "We had a better experience in Mariupol under bombs than there. Everyone tries to leave because it's absolute trash, it's hard to explain. All men have been sent to the Russian army; only handicapped people are left behind. Half of them is sent to fight, and the others are sent to rebuild the destroyed Mariupol."

But at least when Tymofiy reached Donetsk, he was finally able to call his mom again. "I was very mad when I learned that she left Ukraine without us," he said, "I sent her a very angry text. She started calling and explained that they were waiting for us, but they had to flee. So, I calmed myself a bit."

By that time, Tymofiy and his siblings were placed in the Donetsk Tuberculosis hospital.

"The authorities in Donetsk reached out to me demanding children's documents," Olha said, "They told me they wanted to give my children passports of the so-called Donetsk People's Republic. I told them I wouldn't send them any kids' documents, but I did show them the proof that my husband and I were the legal guardians of the children."

"The authorities also told me that if I would not show up personally, they would make children these new passports and give them for adoption to other people," Olha added, "They kept telling this to the kids every day."

According to Ukraine's National Information Bureau, around 12,000 Ukrainian children have been deported to Russia. Most of them are orphans who were separated from their legal guardians and relatives during the Russian occupation. Many children lost their parents recently during Russian strikes on the now-occupied cities, and some children were separated from their parents during the so-called filtration process when their families were trying to flee the war zone.

These children are now placed for adoption in Russia as the Russian parliament passed a new law to speed up the adoption process of Ukrainian children. Many are stranded in Russia while their relatives in Ukraine are denied any communication with them and cannot return them home.

For Olha, rescuing the children was a dilemma. The Donetsk authorities refused to give children to anyone else as a proxy, even when she requested that her brother, who was still in Ukraine, serve as an intermediary guardian. But at the same time, Olha could not leave France where she was registered as a refugee.

"It didn't make sense: here I am, a refugee, fleeing Russia, and then, I return to Russia to get to Donetsk?" she asked, "I didn't even have an international passport at that time. If I left, I'd lose my status, so I wouldn't be able to come back. Then what? Go to Russia and live there with half of my family? If I went to Donetsk, I would not be able to go back to Ukraine or the EU, so my options would be to stay there or mainland Russia. That was a bad perspective."

Donetsk authorities remained unresponsive to Olha and her pleas. The children remained in Donetsk for two months. They could only leave the hospital grounds for a few hours and make a daily call to the parents. Along with the siblings, there were other orphans and children separated from their families in the hospital.

Olha, who was trying to start a new life in France, was slowly losing hope of ever reuniting with her children. However, at the end of April, she received a message from an acquaintance that there was a local volunteer in Donetsk willing to help her.

"I Was Planning to Run Away"

"I still can't believe such people exist," Olha said, "Kind and selfless."

Olha was describing Tetiana Nosach, a Donetsk local activist and founder of shelters for women. Tetiana has been living in Donetsk her whole life. When Russian proxies occupied her city in 2014, she moved to Kyiv for a year. But she missed Donetsk, so she decided to return and stayed there despite the full-scale invasion. She kept her shelters for women there, too.

Tetiana learned about Olha and her children through social media. She reached out and said she could transport the children from Donetsk to Europe if Olha agreed to send her the notarized permission.

"I thought I'd never see my mom again, and I was planning to run away from the hospital when Tetiana showed up," Tymofiy said, "she told me to wait because the authorities would catch me right away. She promised to help."

Together with Tetiana, Tymofiy and his other siblings appealed to the local authorities. With Olha's documents in hand, Tetiana demanded that the children be released from the hospital and given to her. The authorities refused. Tetiana appealed again. This time, all the children went with Tetiana to a special meeting with the authorities. The kids attested to how much they missed their families, and the authorities finally agreed.

Tetiana gathered Tymofiy and his siblings and booked a bus trip for them to go to Moscow. Then, from Moscow, they went to Riga, and from Riga to Berlin. There, Tymofiy's father met them. Tetiana returned to Donetsk while the family drove to France.

"Dad cried, we all cried," Tymofiy recalled.

The family is now reunited and lives in France.

"It was an amazing sensation," Olha recalled when she saw her kids after many months, "I could not hold still."

The whole family has temporary protected status in France, which is granted to Ukrainians who fled Ukraine after February 24. It gives them the right to work and stay in the European Union for the duration of the war.

Olha and her husband have started working in their small town: Olha became a seamstress and learned how to sew even though in Ukraine, she worked as a music teacher. Her husband works as an electrician, and all their children are going to school. They dream of traveling to see the ocean, and they all miss Ukraine.

Losing Your Home to Russia, Twice

A Story of Ukrainians Who Passed Russian Filtration to Flee Occupation

"Our story began in 2014," Iryna says, "We're from Donetsk. We lived practically on the separation line."

Iryna Bilousova is a Ukrainian. Since mid-2022, she is also a refugee after she and her family had to flee Eastern Ukraine from Russian occupation.

For Iryna, this is her second escape. Nine years ago, when Russians first occupied Donetsk and Luhansk, she had to run from her home to the territory controlled by Ukraine. The separation line was the divide between the Ukrainian forces and Russian proxies established in 2014 as Russians attempted to seize more Ukrainian land.

"For three months, we lived in constant fear," Iryna recalled her 2014 experience, "We feared for our lives and for the life of my mom, who is in a wheelchair. When we rushed into the basement, she stayed inside the house. It was very hard."

Iryna is a mother of four children, three young boys, and a teenage daughter. Together with her husband, she took care of them and her elderly mother. When the war in Donbas started, Iryna and her husband could not work anymore because their house was under constant shelling.

"We had no jobs, no money, and no food," the woman recalled, "Thanks to the neighbors, who brought children some food, we could survive. But in September [of 2014], we realized that we could no longer go on like that."

The family decided to flee to the territory controlled by Ukraine. They moved into a village in the Donetsk region, not too far from their previous home in the city of Donetsk. Volunteers helped the family find a house.

"We got a lot of help from the people, especially from Ukrainian soldiers who were stationed nearby," Iryna said, "Things started to improve, and we had a good life for these past eight years."

Everything changed on February 24, 2022.

"At five in the morning, the invaders entered our village," the woman continued, "It was a complete horror. They would shoot from their tanks near our house and then move away from that place. Then, our guys [Ukrainian soldiers] would shoot back to the place where tanks were stationed before."

The family was in the basement when a projectile landed six feet from their house.

"We were almost buried under the rubble," Iryna remembered, "And then, I had to make the hardest decision in my life: to choose between my mom and my children. My mom told me that children needed me and that she'd manage somehow."

Life in Occupation

Iryna's mother could not stay in the basement, and it was difficult to transport her up and down. The older woman stayed in her house while Iryna and her husband would come there between the shelling, feed her, and turn on the stove to make the place a bit warmer.

"Life in occupation is scary," Iryna said, "After Russians entered our village, there were hands, heads, and bodies everywhere. Corpses on the streets. Russians didn't pick them up."

The dead bodies were of Russian soldiers and Ukrainian locals killed by the invading army. The villagers collected the corpses in one spot and covered them with blankets. Iryna recalled seeing how hungry dogs would run around with human parts.

"These monsters [Russian soldiers] went from house to house and took people's cars," the woman proceeded, "Then, when they got drunk, they'd drive the cars around. They also moved into the houses they liked the most and roamed around looking for food. The scariest part was when these drunk beasts — that's the only way to describe them — started coming to our bomb shelter."

Russians were looking for local women in the basements, Iryna explained.

"They'd say things like "You've got so many pretty girls, and we have none," the woman continued, "So we had to hide our daughter. She was seventeen. Our neighbor's daughter was almost raped, but her parents rescued her."

After the talk about "pretty girls", the family decided to flee. They could not enter Ukraine-controlled territory because Russian troops didn't allow people to evacuate there.

"We decided to drive to Russia because my husband had sisters there," Iryna said, "The drive took four days, and my mom barely survived it."

The Donetsk region borders Russia; during a normal pre-war drive, it would take only a few hours to cross the border. However, the family had to make many stops at various checkpoints and avoid getting shot at.

Filtration Camps

The family also had to pass filtration to leave the occupied areas.

"We were in Bezimenne," Iryna said, "We were very lucky and passed filtration in two hours. There were people who stayed in the camp for weeks."

Bezimenne is a village in the Donetsk region on the Azov Sea coast. It is only 20 miles away from Mariupol and less than an hour drive to the Russian border. Since 2014, the village has been under Russian occupation and hosts a notorious filtration camp. Ukrainians who want to flee the occupied areas have to pass a set of tests carried out by Russians; the filtration is used to torture and kill people who don't agree to declare their hatred for Ukraine.

"When we arrived in Bezimenne, we told a Russian soldier that we were with children and a disabled person," Iryna recalled, "The soldier was really rude. He was like: "Who allowed you to talk to me?" I told the guy that we have a disabled person in the car and that she could not move and was in very bad shape."

The woman asked the soldier if she could go through filtration immediately. By that time, there was a line of Ukrainians waiting to pass, and it took days or weeks even to get to the questioning. In the meantime, people had to wait outside.

A higher-ranking soldier showed up and allowed Iryna and her family to go for filtration without waiting in the queue.

"We entered one tent," Iryna said, "It was me, and then, it was my fourteen-year-old son. They asked us questions, and we had to answer by saying that Ukraine was very bad, that the Ukrainian army was very bad, and so on. It was very tough for my husband. A Russian soldier saw that we were from Donetsk originally, and he started yelling at my husband. He called him a "f***er" and yelled at him for not joining the Russian army. The guy was screaming things like, "You went to Ukropia! [derogatory for Ukraine]. And I have to protect you? We will send your family away, and we will take you with us!"

The questioning lasted for around an hour, with Russian soldiers threatening her husband and telling him they'd beat him up.

"When my husband was done, he was white as a ghost," Iryna recalled, "His hands still shake as he remembers that. But thank God, they let us pass. They checked our phones and allowed us to go."

The family's experience with filtration is better than most people who went through it; many are stripped naked and tortured if they have any Ukraine-themed tattoos or don't answer the questions the way they are expected.

"You have to tell them what they want to hear," Iryna explained, "About Russia, about Ukraine, about the war. That's the only way to pass."

Escaping Russia

"We spent two months in Russia," Iryna continued, "We needed money to move farther, and my mom needed time to come back to her senses. She almost lost her mind during the occupation because she lived alone without any electricity."

Iryna and her husband managed to find some temporary jobs and raised a bit of money to leave Russia. They started looking for buses and private drivers. The prices were too high.

"That's when I found the volunteers," Iryna said, "And they helped! Thanks to them, we are no longer shaking whenever we hear some noise, and we're starting to get used to the sound of planes and helicopters."

The woman is referring to mushrooming civil society groups that help deported Ukrainians escape Russia and enter neighboring EU countries. Volunteers—mostly Ukrainians based in Ukraine and Baltic countries—connect with Ukrainians via Telegram and help them with transportation, money, and advice.

"A volunteer coordinator reached out to us and helped us drive from Rostov-on-Don to Estonia," Iryna said, "She was with us on the line throughout the entire journey. The coordinator sent us the safest route because we were driving with a disabled person."

When the family was crossing the Russian-Estonian border, they were also questioned for a few hours by the Russian officers. The questions were similar to the ones they heard during the filtration process.

"Russians asked us why we wanted to leave Russia instead of staying there," Iryna added, "But this questioning was less scary and without yelling."

From Estonia, the family drove to Germany where they applied for refugee status. In early January, they were informed that their refugee camp is going to shut down in mid-March.

"They told us that the land was sold, so we have to look for another housing," Iryna said, "Those who can't find anything can go to another refugee camp, which is in the suburbs. But it's not as good, and they wouldn't accept my mom there. They wanted to send her into a nursing home for disabled people instead. That's why we're running around now and looking for housing because I don't want to separate from my mom."

"So, this is what it's like to live in Germany as a refugee," she added, "It's not all that great, but at least, it is peaceful here. So, we can manage."

Besides Iryna's family, the camp hosted many other Ukrainians. Iryna made many friends who are in a similar situation to hers.

"The main thing is that we're all alive and together," she concluded, "So all is going to be okay."

Surviving a Russian Missile Strike

The Harrowing Narrative of How a Ukrainian Surgeon Rescued His Wife after a Deadly Missile Strike on Their Home

February 2023

"Some of our neighbors survived, but most of them died," said Olha, "They lived on the lower levels where everything was destroyed." Olha Botvinova survived a deadly attack on a residential building in Dnipro, Eastern Ukraine, on Jan. 14, when Russians launched a missile attack against the city. One of the missiles hit Olha's building, killing 46 residents, including six children.

"Everything was burning, everything was full of smoke," Olha remembered, "Explosions continued, and we heard many screams. People screamed really loud at first, but soon, there were fewer and fewer voices."

It was because she was with her husband, a surgeon, that Olha survived. He managed to slow her bleeding while the couple waited more than three hours in the nearly destroyed building before rescuers finally got to them.

"It was like a second birth," Olha said, of emerging from the destruction.

Escaping the "Russian World"

Olha and her husband, Yevhen, are originally from Donetsk, which was once one of the biggest cities in Eastern Ukraine with nearly a million residents. Olha worked there as a bank manager, and Yevhen worked as a surgeon in a local clinic.

In 2014, however, things changed for the family. That spring, Russia annexed the Crimean Peninsula in Ukraine and launched a war in Donbas, which affected the city of Donetsk and nearby areas. Russia-affiliated proxies proclaimed a so-called Donetsk People's Republic effectively separating the region from the rest of Ukraine.

"We decided to leave and moved to Kherson," said Yevhen, "I found a job there, and Olha started working as a trainer for entrepreneurs. She was always interested in psychology."

The couple lived in Kherson for eight years. The city is in Southern Ukraine, close to the Crimean Peninsula. It was the first and only regional capital that Russia managed to occupy since the start of its full-scale invasion of Ukraine in 2022.

So, the couple had to flee again.

"When Russians occupied Kherson, I managed to evacuate Olha right away," Yevhen recalled, "I drove her to Dnipro and returned home to help people. But quickly, Russians started putting a lot of pressure on the hospital. They were forcing us to sign documents that we were now working in Russia. We were also supposed to start using Russian money. Of course, I was against that, so I left for good."

The escape was difficult.

"I had to sleep in the fields to leave the occupied area," the man said, "It took a long night to pass the Russian-controlled area."

When Yevhen finally reached Dnipro, he started to work there as a surgeon. Olha was already settled in the city. In June, the couple rented out a one-bedroom apartment in a residential area in Dnipro.

It was that apartment that was hit on Jan. 14.

Surviving the Attack

"It was Saturday, a day off, but I had to work," Yevhen recalled, "I got home after work, and Olha was just finishing her stuff. I felt good, happy even, and I didn't expect anything bad to happen so soon."

On that day, their building had little electricity, so it started getting cold. Olha was annoyed because she could not work as her internet was too weak. She could not even call her team to finish a work call.

"I remember Yevhen calling me to the living room," the woman said, "He was under the blanket on the coach, and he wanted me to come and rest with him. Ten minutes before the attack I got under the blanket and hugged him really tight."

The next thing the couple remembers were explosions.

"When the missile hit, I saw how the window frame flew over me," Yevhen said, "It hit the other side of the room. Glass, walls, and rubble: all started falling on us."

The man remembers: he had no panic. He checked on his wife: she had an injury and was bleeding from her temple.

"There was a lot of blood, and it looked bad, but I am a surgeon, and I saw that it was not too deep," Yevhen said, "I made some bandages and pressed on the wound to reduce bleeding."

The couple had an emergency suitcase for crisis situations. They worried that there would be new explosions and so they wanted to leave the building right away.

"When we tried to exit the apartment, we saw that there were no more stairs, and everything was too damaged to go down," Yevhen said, "So we decided to stay where we were. I knew that if the kitchen floor would hold, then the rescuers would get to us."

"We sat on the kitchen floor for three hours," Olha recalled, "My husband would come to what used to be the window and send light signals with a flashlight. He was showing that we were still here and that we were alive."

The rescuers managed to get the couple out of the building. Olha lost consciousness on her way to the hospital.

"I woke up already in the clinic," the woman recalled, "The doctor told me that we were blessed to have survived that attack. There were many of our neighbors in that hospital, some of them died, and some of them survived. It was very hard."

"My fight thought when I woke up was: Thank God that we're alive," Olha continued, "I was crying and in shock. My body was shaking. But the next day, it was very different. I could not be happy to be alive because I knew so many people died."

The couple spent ten days in the hospital and had to go through rehabilitation.

While in the hospital, Olha and Yevhen learned that their apartment in Kherson was also destroyed. On Jan. 15, a day after the deadly attack on Dnipro, Russia launched an attack on residential areas in Kherson.

Despite that, the couple remained optimistic.

"The most important thing is that we're alive," Yevhen said.

"I want us to improve our health and return back to our community," Olha concluded, "I want to be useful to people and work toward victory."

Her Child Was Deported to Russia

How a Ukrainian Servicewoman Returned Her Daughter

March 2023

"It was shock, and fury, and fear all at once," says Kseniia Lebedenko, "I just could not process that they sent my child to Russia."

Kseniia sighs as she says it: perhaps, to calm herself, or maybe, to shake off the memories of that difficult experience. It's been a month since she was reunited with her daughter, 11-year-old Eva, after nearly a year of separation. She is still very angry about what happened.

"They could not just take her there without my permission," the woman proceeds, "I almost lost hope."

Kseniia's pro-Russian brother brought her child to Russia and refused to return Eva to her mother. Kseniia, a military medic in the Ukrainian army, could not get the child herself.

"I was contemplating about traveling to Russia to get Eva back," she says, "I knew I might not return, but I'd try and bring her home."

After months of struggles, Kseniia was finally able to see her child back in Ukraine.

Losing Contact

Kseniia is a military medic with Ukraine's Armed Forces. In her early forties, with a round, motherly face, she is an experienced medical professional who has worked in hospitals for years.

The woman spent most of her life in her native Vovchansk, a quiet little town only 5 miles from the Russian border. Divorced, Kseniia raised her daughter as a single mom with support from her elderly parents. Her brother lived nearby with his wife and two children.

A month before Russia launched its full-scale invasion, Kseniia changed jobs. She moved to Kharkiv, a one-hour drive from her hometown, and became a military medic.

"In late January, I signed my contract, and I started to serve with the Ukrainian army," the woman recalls.

Her daughter stayed in Vovchansk with her grandparents. As Russians launched their full-scale invasion of Ukraine on February 24, 2022, Vovchansk was one of the first places that fell.

The quiet town turned eerie during the occupation. Russian troops quickly cut off all the communication Vovchansk had with the rest of Ukraine.

"I could not get to them," Kseniia says, "It was a complete disconnection."

For months, she tried to reach her family back home, but it was nearly impossible.

"They had no cellphone connection and no internet," the woman continues, "They barely had any electricity. Whenever I tried to call, I could not get through to them. It was very hard to communicate, very hard to take it in."

Throughout spring and summer, Kseniia combined her work as a military medic with her attempts to rescue Eva from the occupation.

"I was serving near Izium in the Kharkiv region, and I was looking for ways to bring Eva to Ukraine-controlled territories," she continues, "But my family was not very supportive of the idea. Basically, they turned pro-Russian while I was serving with the Ukrainian army. I could not communicate with them very much and knew little what was going on, so I could not rescue my daughter."

By that time, Eva was staying with Kseniia's brother.

"I was begging my family to give Eva back to me," Kseniia says, pain in her voice, "I told them I could find volunteers who'd drive Eva to safety in Ukraine. But they didn't agree."

Kseniia didn't know this back then, but her brother supported the occupation. On September 7, he became one of the first locals to receive a Russian passport. The video of him getting citizenship was widely circulated on Russian propaganda channels.

"I was really waiting for this moment," Andriy Lebedenko said to Russian journalists during the citizenship ceremony, "It's like my second birthday. We are all the same people; we are all Russians."

A week after Andriy became a Russian citizen, Ukrainian troops liberated Vovchansk.

"They Took My Daughter to Russia"

Around the time that Russians retreated from her hometown, Kseniia was fighting on another front. With her unit, she was deployed near Bakhmut, where some of the heaviest fighting took place.

"In September, I got wounded. A brain injury," Kseniia explains, "There was artillery fire against our positions. My phone was destroyed, so I had no contacts, no phone numbers. I could not call my parents right away, and I could not go there because of my injury."

Kseniia's acquaintances traveled to Vovchansk to get Eva after the city was liberated. From them, the woman learned that her daughter was not in the country anymore. Andriy took Eva and his family to Russia before Ukrainian forces entered the town.

"I was very angry and shocked, and afraid," Kseniia says, "I could not believe they took her out of Ukraine illegally. They had no right to do that without my permission."

"Why didn't he go to a territory controlled by Ukraine?" the medic asks bitterly. And, without waiting for an answer, "Well, what's the point when he already got the Russian passport?"

Through her mother, Kseniia got Andriy's phone number.

"I started calling him," she says, "I begged him to let me talk to Eva, but he refused."

Andriy moved to the Belgorod region, not far from the Ukrainian border. He bought a small house there and established his family—and his niece—in a small village two hours away from Vovchansk.

"I asked Andriy to return Eva to me," Kseniia goes on, "I wanted to talk to her, but he would find all kinds of excuses. This went on for months."

As soon as the medic was released from the hospital, she resigned from her position to be able to return Eva. Kseniia went to the local police and reported that her daughter was illegally taken to Russia.

The police connected Kseniia with volunteers who focus on returning deported Ukrainian children from Russia.

Since the start of the full-scale invasion, Russia deported at least 12,000 Ukrainian children although Russian sources claim that the number is at least 700,000. Many children are orphans, taken away from their legal guardians and relatives. Some were orphaned recently when their parents were killed during the occupation. Some got separated, like Eva.

Russian parliament passed a new law that allows for the speedy adoption of Ukrainian children. According to the Russian authorities, at least 1,000 of them have been adopted already. Ukrainian guardians are denied information on children's whereabouts, so unless a child finds a way to communicate with family back home, it is nearly impossible to track and return the kids. Often, when the parents appeal to Russian authorities to get their children back, they get a refusal.

In Ukraine, volunteers help the families return the kids if they already know where they are. Volunteers create the safest route and help with transportation and documents. Most times, relatives have to drive to Russia to get the children themselves.

For Kseniia, this was tricky.

"I served in the Ukrainian army, so I couldn't go to Russia," she says, "And my brother did not want to cooperate at all. He didn't want to return Eva or tell me where they were. I felt like I was failing, and I could not get to him. There were moments when I was on the verge of giving up."

Eva's Home

Eva was in Russia from September to December. After three months of non-stop calling, Andriy finally agreed to return the child home.

"Volunteers helped me prepare a document that granted power of attorney to another woman who was in a similar situation," Kseniia explains, "She went to Russia to get her child, and she brought Eva with her."

On December 17, Kseniia finally saw her daughter.

"I have not seen her for almost a year," Kseniia says, tears in her eyes, "I don't remember how we met again. It was just too much for me, so blurry. Too many emotions."

Mother and daughter moved to the Poltava region in the North of Ukraine. They took Kseniia's parents with them.

"We cannot go back to Vovchansk now," she explains, "It is too dangerous because there is constant shelling from the Russian side. The town is on the verge of a humanitarian catastrophe."

In their new home, Kseniia takes care of her parents and spends as much time as she can with Eva. She doesn't talk to her brother anymore.

"There is nothing I have to say to him," she sighs, "We have very different values. I don't know how he could sell his country like that. It is bad, and it upsets me very much that this happened to my family. I don't know how it happened, but it did."

Kseniia hopes to return to the Armed Forces soon. But for now, she's staying home; Eva and her parents need her.

"I am very happy she is home," Kseniia says, "I was afraid she'd not return. But now, she is here, and everything will be all right."

Fighting for Her Fiancé's Legacy in Ukraine

Grief Made Her Follow Her Late Fiancé into the Ukrainian Army, but Seeking Vengeance on the Front Lines Isn't Bringing Her Peace

April 2023

"It was a friend who told me that Oleksandr died," Anastasiia said, "I don't remember too well what happened next. I just screamed and screamed."

This is how Anastasiia Blyshchyk learned that her fiancé was killed in action. It was May 4, 2022.

"For three days, I was in denial, hoping that it was a lie," Anastasiia recalled, "Then, I got a text from a military medic from Oleksandr's unit. The text said: 'I am sorry I could not save him.' It was the worst thing that could have happened to me."

Anastasiia's fiancé, Oleksandr Makhov, volunteered to serve in the Ukrainian army on February 24, 2022, the first day of Russia's full-scale invasion. He was already an experienced soldier: He had served back in 2015 during the war in Donbas.

Both Anastasiia and Oleksandr worked as journalists. They met in the office of their TV station and fell in love. Anastasiia was the one who accompanied Oleksandr to the conscription office on February 24, 2022.

After her fiancé's death, the woman surrounded herself with family and work. For a few months, she tried to navigate her loss by overworking herself until, in July 2022, she went to the conscription office herself—and joined the Ukrainian army.

She now serves near the Belarusian border.

"I did not come to the frontline to die," Anastasiia said, "There is war in my country. We cannot win if we all sit and wait for others to protect us. As we speak, someone is getting a phone call that their loved ones have been killed in action while protecting their country heroically. This is hell."

At War

"I remember the first day of the full-scale war," Anastasiia recalled, "I was in Kyiv, and I fell asleep at 3 am. I had some bad feelings. I expected that the full-scale invasion would happen, but I, like most people, didn't know that we would be bombed right away."

Back in February 2022, Anastasiia was working as a journalist at a national TV station. Her fiancé, Oleksandr, was her colleague, and on February 24, 2022, he was in Donbas, a region in Eastern Ukraine, part of which has been under Russian occupation since 2014. He was there to report, but he also knew the area well. Oleksandr served in the East with the Ukrainian army since 2015, when he volunteered to defend his native land. Originally from Donbas himself, Oleksandr's hometown has been under occupation since 2014.

"Oleksandr called me early on February 24," Anastasiia continued, "He told me: 'Anastasiia, Putin announced a full-scale invasion.' I started calling all my family. My parents were in the Kherson region at that time, which is 50 miles from Crimea. My mom thought that I was just very sleepy and didn't know what I was saying. But after she hung up, she heard the explosions and the movement of Russian tanks. She heard missiles above her head which were flying to destroy Ukrainian cities."

The Kherson region, which links the annexed Crimean Peninsula with mainland Ukraine, was one of the first Ukrainian territories to be occupied in 2022.

"I later called my sister in Zaporizhzhia, and they also heard the missiles," Anastasiia recalled.

At the time, she was recovering from the coronavirus, so she had been in isolation for a week. The woman left her apartment to get some food and cash. Oleksandr asked her to host some evacuees from the Bakhmut area, so she prepared for their arrival. Then she went to work, carrying her emergency backpack. She was sent to cover any news coming out of the President's Office.

"We heard some reassurances from them, and then, I asked: How can everything be ok if there are Russian tanks in my native Kherson region?"

A few hours later, Oleksandr returned to Kyiv.

"It felt so normal and cozy with him," Anastasiia remembered, "He picked me up from work, he showered, and we ate in our small cozy kitchen. I was checking the news all the time. Oleksandr told me: 'Put away your phone, please, I want to talk to you because I am going to go to the conscription office.' I said: 'Wait, you've been on the road all day. Why don't you sleep at home, and tomorrow morning, we will both go to the conscription office.' And he answered: 'I won't be able to sleep because good people are dying there. I have to be there.' Then, in that kitchen where we spent our evenings, chatting about our days and future plans, he hugged me tight, and he said: 'Forgive me for everything. I love you.'"

Oleksandr didn't take any of the food Anastasiia tried to put in his backpack. He said: "We've got food in the army; it is not 2014." Anastasiia still managed to slip a chocolate bar into his pocket. Then, the couple walked to the conscription office. The public transport didn't work, and all the taxis that passed were full.

"February 24 was very warm," Anastasiia said "Oleksandr took off his jacket, saying he regretted taking all his warm clothes. Nobody predicted that March would be so cold and snowy and that the chocolate bar I gave him would be his only food for two days."

Oleksandr entered the conscription office, and Anastasiia waited outside and watched groups of Ukrainian volunteers being led to the buses. They were all yelling: "Glory to Ukraine. Glory to heroes. Putin is a f***er."

"I watched how people were hugging and kissing each other as they were sending their loved ones to war," Anastasiia remembered, "Then, Oleksandr got out. He told me: 'Remember: 95th assault brigade.' This is where he was assigned to. I asked him: 'So are you going to leave right now?' He said: 'No, I will stay with you for a bit.' He held me really tight. I wanted to say something to him, but he said: 'No, wait,' and held me tighter. And then, he asked me something very surprising. He said: 'Will you wait for me?' I said: 'Of course, I will wait for you.' He repeated that he loved me and asked for forgiveness again. And then, Oleksandr left."

Anastasiia went home alone. She stayed with friends who lived nearby because she did not want to be by herself in the apartment. On that night, there were big explosions just outside Kyiv, but nonetheless, she somehow managed to sleep.

"Emotionally, I was drained," she said, "My parents were in the Kherson region under Russian occupation, and Oleksandr went to war."

Loss

Anastasiia became a news editor after Oleksandr's deployment. She wanted to keep a regular schedule so she would have free time to track down ammunition to send to her fiancé and support any other way she could. Oleksandr convinced Anastasiia that the Ukrainian army had everything, but nobody knew then how many people had signed up. Before the full-scale invasion, the Ukrainian army was around 250,000 people. Now, it is about 700,000. She spent the spring months getting updates from Oleksandr, working, and volunteering.

Then, on May 4, 2022, Anastasiia received that fateful call: her fiancé was killed in battle.

For three days, she was in shock.

"On day four, I got a death certificate from the military office, which included the time and location of Oleksandr's death," Anastasiia said, "And on the fifth day, I buried him. Burying someone young who was killed at war is very scary. I was hoping he was still alive. To be honest, I still hope that someone would tell me that it was all a mistake. My brain understands that Oleksandr died, but I cannot accept the fact that it is forever."

The day after the burial, Anastasiia went to Zaporizhzhia to stay with her sister.

"When he died, I had no reasons to live," she remembered, "We had so many plans, but then, in one day, the plans were gone. There was nothing. I would wake up and not know why I was there on this planet. What's next? I had never experienced anything like that. We all need plans, but I had none of that. I lost all my senses.

This lasted for three weeks. It was the worst period of my life, those three weeks after we buried Oleksandr."

In June 2022, Anastasiia gathered her strength and returned to the capital.

"I filled my schedule with lots of work, meetings, and tasks so I could come home as tired as possible and fall asleep," she said, "If I had any energy left, I would not be able to sleep. This is when I realized I wanted to join the army. So, I went to the mountains to get some energy from the trip. Oleksandr and I were supposed to go there together this summer. I took his Ukrainian flag with me; it was signed by his fellow soldiers back in 2016 when he first served. When I returned from that trip to Kyiv, I started collecting all the documents and enlisted."

Anastasiia joined the army on Sept. 4, 2022, three months after Oleksandr died.

When she was mobilized, Anastasiia's friends asked her: "What would Oleksandr think about it?" Anastasiia's answer was: "On February 25, when I wanted to sign up for the first time, he supported me."

In the Army

"Right now, I am stationed near the border with Belarus where I serve as a Press officer of the 47th Assault brigade 'Magura,'" Anastasiia explained, "Prior to this, I served in the 113th unit in the Kharkiv region."

It was with the 113th unit that Anastasiia entered liberated Izium in mid-September 2022. There, she found the very place where Oleksandr was killed.

"I wanted to serve in the Kharkiv region because this is where he died," Anastasiia said, "It happened in a village called Dovhenke near Izium. I went there. I asked Oleksandr's comrades to describe the exact location. The village is huge and nearly destroyed, and I had no connection there. However, whether thanks to intuition or some other sense, I found that spot."

Anastasiia was there five months to the day after his death.

Now, nearly a year later, she is still on the frontline where she works as a press officer for the army.

"I realized that given my journalistic experience, I can do what I can to make journalists' work more comfortable so they can cover things better," she said.

"I want the world to see the crimes committed by Russia, and I want to help journalists document these crimes."

"We are all soldiers regardless of our job title," Anastasiia added, "We have to know how to use arms, and we have to be ready to fight when needed. When the enemy attacks, it does not really matter if you're a cook, a medic, a press officer, or anything else. Everyone is trained to be prepared for everything, so we learned how to shoot and act in all kinds of situations."

Anastasiia experienced all the hardships the soldiers endure: lack of showers, fitful sleep, and a life without the amenities people take for granted during peace.

"The hardest part is seeing your friends killed," she said, "I thought that when I'd come to the frontline and get my revenge, it would make it easier for me. But even though I have seen dead Russians rotting away abandoned by their own soldiers, it does not bring Oleksandr back. Most people don't understand this about war."

"People who lost their loved ones at this war feel differently toward death," the soldier explained, "I am not afraid of getting killed, but I don't want to die because I have a lot of plans that are connected to Oleksandr. I am afraid of how my death would affect my parents and my sister. I am afraid for them, but I am not afraid of the concept of death. How can I be afraid after what I lived through? I fear for my relatives because I know what it is like to lose someone you love."

The Future

While Anastasiia was recovering after Oleksandr's death and enlisting with the army, her parents were under Russian occupation. Originally from the left bank of the Kherson region, they managed to flee to Ukraine-controlled territory in September 2022. Anastasiia visited them for a few days in Zaporizhzhia where they live now.

"This is when they learned that I was serving the Ukrainian nation," the woman said.

"I spent my youth in the Kherson region, and I left it when I went to the university," Anastasiia recalled, "I knew classmates and locals from there. Now, many of these people wave Russian flags. I understand that after the liberation, there would be investigations, but those will mostly affect occupation authorities and collaborators. But what would happen to those waving Russian flags? I am convinced that nothing would happen to them. They would just wait it out quietly. However, pro-Ukrainian locals, who were resisting and were disgusted by the Russian flags, will remind them of everything. They will remind them with words and glances, and those other people would not be able to lift their gaze. They would be ashamed and afraid to go to jail."

I sense the change in Anastasiia as she says this. Throughout our conversation, we had to take breaks when it got too emotional. But now, Anastasiia's voice is strong and determined.

"The victory of Ukraine is not when we return to the 1991 borders," she said, "The victory will take place when each of us will change, and we will understand that our country is strong, and our language is the most powerful weapon, when we overcome corruption, and when we restore all of our destroyed buildings."

"The most important thing is to be grateful to all our heroes for giving their lives while fighting for Ukraine," Anastasiia concluded, "I do not want people to forget. We must live and remember. Even after the war, we will have our army, and we need to have respect for all the soldiers. Every hero who died was protecting us, and we will protect and defend their memory."

For Anastasiia, this is personal: She wants to preserve her memory of Oleksandr. Her fiancé was awarded the Order for Courage posthumously by President Volodymyr Zelenskyy.

There is also a street in the capital of Ukraine that is named after Oleksandr, and there is another street in Izium that was liberated thanks to soldiers like him. Anastasiia vows to protect Oleksandr's legacy as she keeps serving Ukraine.

"Proud Ukrainian with Nigerian Roots"

Alice Zhuravel Is Combatting Misinformation by Elevating the Narratives of Diverse Ukrainians

May 2023

"My identity journey was not straightforward," Alice smiled, "It was complex and confusing at times, and it took some years to figure out."

Alice Zhuravel is a radiant young woman. In her mid-twenties, charming, she exudes confidence and trust. In a coffee place in her native Kharkiv, Eastern Ukraine, Alice shared her thoughts on what it was like growing up with a mixed background and how diversity is perceived in Ukraine now.

"I came to accept myself fully," she told me, "I embraced my identity as a proud Ukrainian with Nigerian roots, and it helped me tremendously."

"I used to wonder about people's origins and what it meant for their identities," Alice added, "I embrace the idea of diversity and that people of different backgrounds identify as Ukrainians because they are born and raised here."

"The war especially made me want to highlight the diversity that is here, in Ukraine, and that's why I decided to launch my project," she continued, "I want to show the true Ukraine to the people who've never been here and showcase how the racist tropes around Ukraine are false."

Alice Zhuravel is the founder of Tozhsamist—which means "identity" in Ukrainian. It is a digital platform that collects testimonies of Ukrainians of color. Through personal stories, diverse Ukrainians are trying to break the Russian narratives about Ukraine, which portray their native country as racist and intolerant.

"We're decolonizing Ukraine for us and for the world," Alice said.

Reflecting on Identity

"I was always interested in diversity because it is relevant to me personally," Alice explained. As a Ukrainian with Nigerian roots, she started to notice some differences between herself and others when going to school. "There was no discrimination toward me or anything that made me feel excluded," she said, "I did not feel any difference from other kids until I started paying more attention to my hair. In Ukraine in the nineties, there were few products suited for African hair. When I saw my classmates have small braids, I started realizing this difference as I had a big Afro."

At first, Alice did not like being different. She relaxed her hair and tried to blend in as much as possible. However, as she grew up, her attitude toward differences—such as skin color, hair, or diverse heritage—changed. She started listening to hip-hop music and reading about African cultures, which helped her understand her value and uniqueness. "I started wearing my Afro proudly," Alice smiled, "As a kid, I never thought I would do it, but as an adult, I loved my natural hair. I accepted it because it was mine. I accepted myself fully."

At the same time, Alice still struggled with her Ukrainian identity. Growing up so close to the Russian border, she rarely used Ukrainian outside school or work. Her attitudes toward Ukrainian culture and language also started to change as Russia first invaded Ukraine in 2014. "I remember telling my mom that if something were to happen in Kharkiv, if Russia were to invade it, then I would immediately switch to Ukrainian," she said. "So, it has been 14 months since I speak Ukrainian all the time."

When Alice decided to share her identity journey with the world, she received many messages from fellow Ukrainians praising her work. Many came forward with their testimonies of growing up as Ukrainians of color or digging up long-forgotten family ties to other cultures and countries.

Race and Identity

Ukraine is a predominantly white country, although its demographics have changed dramatically in the last century.

Ukrainians were cleansed during the Stalin repressions and throughout the entire Soviet period; at least 4 million ethnic Ukrainians were killed. In addition, Communist leadership deported Indigenous Crimean Tatars from the Crimean Peninsula to various countries in Central Asia. Other ethnic groups — such as Jews and Poles — were displaced, killed during the Second World War, or Russified.

Ethnic Russians were instead brought in large numbers to Ukraine, and the Russification of Ukraine intensified. While Ukrainian was still widely used, Russian became the main language of politics and decision-making.

It was in this environment, where all were expected to identify as "Soviet citizens" and use Russian as a common denominator, that new immigrants started coming to Ukraine. In addition to residents of other then-Soviet republics from Central Asia and the South Caucasus, many Africans arrived in Ukraine. After the decolonization of many African states, young professionals and students from USSR-friendly countries came to the Soviet Union to study, work, or just visit. While many have returned home, others chose to settle in a new country.

Before Russia's full-scale invasion, almost five million Ukrainians were immigrants, meaning they were born outside of Ukraine; Africans were the second biggest group arriving in Ukraine in the past ten years after Asians. Black Ukrainians comprise less than 1% of Ukraine's current population, and most reside in urban areas. In addition, there are approximately 30,000 Africans studying in Ukraine. The number shrank by one-third when the Russo-Ukrainian war started.

While Ukraine's population remains predominantly white, the country's pre-war's flow of tourism and immigrants made Ukrainians more receptive toward diversity.

As Alice put it, "Ukraine's lack of colonization of other countries has contributed to its relative lack of various ethnic diversity compared to others." Yet, as the activist highlighted, "Ukraine cannot be characterized as monocultural or monoethnic" because many cultures are represented there.

"Russian propaganda portrayed race in Ukraine in a very negative light," Alice said, "However, this is not the reality."

Amplifying Diverse Voices

Alice is a historian by training. Throughout her life, she lived and worked across Ukraine, doing art projects, designing strategies, and finally moving into research.

"In the summer of 2022, I started analyzing what kind of news people from all over the world were receiving about Ukraine," she said, "Lots of Russian narratives were claiming that Ukraine was racist and Nazi. For Ukrainians, this information is obviously false, so we just ignore it. However, for a lot of foreigners, this propaganda really worked."

Alice realized that many people outside of Ukraine formed a very negative image of her country. Even though many have never been to Ukraine or only learned about it in 2022, lots of foreigners pictured Ukraine as racist, intolerant, and aggressive toward people of color.

Alice does not deny that there is racism in Ukraine; however, she rejects that it is systematic or that it is a mainstream social attitude. "Just because there are individuals who are racist in Ukraine does not mean that they represent the entire nation," she explained, "There are racists in the US and elsewhere, but we don't just assume that the entire country is like that. I mean, if someone from a certain country steal, does it mean everyone is a thief there?"

Alice's native city, Kharkiv, has attracted a large number of foreign students, many from Africa and the Middle East, but thousands fled the country when the full-scale invasion started. There is a similar situation in other major university cities. International tourism nearly disappeared because of the ongoing war and negative propaganda.

"This is huge because this influences the situation on the information front, and it also influences our stance in the cultural and social spaces," she said, "I want people from across the world to be able to visit Ukraine and enjoy it. Due to Russian propaganda, we may not get foreigners coming and exploring Ukraine."

To tackle this situation, Alice is sharing testimonies of non-white Ukrainians. She collected stories from African and Latin Ukrainians as well as testimonies of Crimean Tatars, an Indigenous population from the Crimean Peninsula.

"It is very difficult to work with disinformation," Alice continued, "My only tool is to show true stories of diverse Ukrainians like me. I do not hide anything. I show the reality of Ukraine, and if people keep on disbelieving me, the only thing I can do is to invite them to Ukraine to see for themselves."

What Narrative Can Do

"While collecting people's stories, I got to discuss with other Ukrainians of color the difference between ignorance or curiosity and racism," Alice said, "Very often, these two get mixed up, but it is crucial to separate them."

For example, Alice used to notice people checking out her hair. Once, a little girl approached her and asked if she could touch it. Alice laughed it off.

"If adult people act this way, they are ignorant and rude," the woman reflected, "However, they do it not because they are racist, but because they do not understand some ethical boundaries."

Alice hopes that her work will encourage more Ukrainians to reflect on their past and present and appreciate diversity as a part of their country. "I would like to help society become more diversity-friendly and respectful. Diversity is great, and we need to celebrate it," she said, "We need both state policy toward diversity and greater understanding and respect toward inclusion and human rights. We need to start working on this now, so when Ukraine wins, this approach will be a part of our reconstruction."

Alice also aspires to spur more discussions on colonialism and postcolonialism in Ukraine, a country badly affected by Russian imperialism and still coming to terms with its collective trauma. She started paying more attention to the way the Ukrainian language is being used to revive Ukrainian identity and how former Russian speakers like herself are switching to Ukrainian in massive numbers. Ukrainians are also embracing historical figures who were

demonized during Soviet times and demanding more representation in the world — such as fighting against mislabeling Ukrainian
artists as Russians.

"Through my conversations with Crimean Tatars, I learned so
much about their history and about their deportations," Alice said,
"It was heartbreaking to hear the stories of families forcefully taken
away from their homeland. One person I interviewed told me that
while her grandfather was in Vienna fighting in the Red Army, his
family was being deported to Central Asia."

"Having these conversations and sharing these stories really
helped put colonialism onto the central stage," Alice added, "The
same practices are being used right now, and we should ask ourselves why this imperialism is still allowed."

"We as a society need to understand what was Russified and
colonized, so we can get rid of these stamps," she concluded,
"While times have changed, Russia's colonialist methods have
not."

Reporting from Bakhmut

The Independent Journalists behind Free Radio Continue to Report from inside Occupied Ukraine

May 2023

When Anastasiia Shybiko turned 21 in May of 2017, she moved a thousand miles across the country to do something completely different. A journalism student, she was full of youthful maximalism, and she wanted to launch a new and daring project. So, she packed her things and traveled all the way from Lviv, Western Ukraine, to Bakhmut, right next to the invading Russian army. Back then, Russian troops maintained a low-scale war in Donbas, an Eastern Ukrainian region on the border with Russia.

There, with a team of like-minded young journalists, she started the city's first independent media: Free Radio.

Now, five years later, Anastasiia and her colleagues are displaced across Ukraine. The city of Bakhmut, a place that has been the center of their reporting, is nearly gone, wiped out during a months-long battle of attrition. Most residents are gone, too, finding refuge in other parts of Ukraine or the world.

Yet, Free Radio continues working, covering news from Bakhmut and beyond.

"Our main objective, for now, is to survive," Anastasiia said, "And then, we want to expand to more areas outside of Bakhmut and cover the entire Donetsk region."

"We know that people in the occupation listen to us," the journalist added, "They want to know what's happening, and they know they can trust us to tell the truth."

"So, we're already thinking how to report and reintegrate those parts of Ukraine that are still occupied," the woman added, "These territories will be freed soon, and we will need to talk to people there as soon as it happens."

Bracing for Change

"Our team consists of sixteen people now," Anastasiia told me, "It went through a lot of transformations, and many people came and went."

"We started with our idea in 2017, but we consider our birthday the first time we went on air," she added, "That was April 5, 2018."

I am somewhat puzzled by Anastasiia. She looks familiar and sounds nothing like an Easterner with her typical Western Ukrainian accent.

"The thing is, I am not from Bakhmut at all," she laughed at my confusion, "I am originally from the Lviv region, and I studied journalism at Lviv University. I started school in 2013, and two months later, the Revolution of Dignity started."

The revolution, which ousted corrupt pro-Russian President Viktor Yanukovych, brought more than a million people to the capital. They protested for months to make the president reverse back on his anti-EU policies and then resign. The revolution turned bloody when government forces opened fire on peaceful protesters, something that had not happened in independent Ukraine before. When Yanukovych lost his grip on power in February 2014, he fled to Russia; soon after, Russian troops invaded the Donbas region in Eastern Ukraine and annexed the Southern peninsula of Crimea.

"When I went to Kyiv to protest, I saw how important journalism was," Anastasiia recalled of that memorable time, "So I started working as a professional journalist, and in September of 2014, I had my first assignment in the East. After this, I regularly covered the war in Donbas."

Anastasiia admits that by the time she graduated from uni, she was already burnt out and considered quitting journalism. However, in 2017, she got a call from a friend who volunteered in the East.

"He said to me: 'You worked in the East before. Let's go back there together to create a local radio,'" the journalist remembered, "So I thought: "Let's do it!"

Challenging the Status Quo

A team of like-minded volunteers came to Bakhmut and started working on their project. Many were not from the East and did not understand the local dynamics. However, it turned out for the best.

"A lot of locals told us: "This isn't your Kyiv or Lviv, you cannot criticize certain people here," Anastasiia recalled, "However, we were young and naive, and we came to Bakhmut with our values and ideas of change. We didn't know who to fear, so we didn't. We investigated everyone, and we were and remain independent."

Launching a free media was tough in an environment where many news channels were owned or influenced by businesses or politicians; and where few dared to run local-themed investigations. As Anastasiia and her team realized, the war was not the only problem in this part of the country. There was corruption, Russia's information warfare, and a lack of quality media to challenge the status quo.

"We trained a lot of locals who later became our correspondents," the reporter recalled, "We helped them become better journalists than those who worked for years in the Donetsk region. They did amazing investigative work, and it is a huge achievement training these former economists, activists, and so on."

Over time, the team grew and expanded to a digital platform and an FM radio station. It increased its reach outside of Bakhmut and to Ukrainian territories that Russia occupied in 2014, which are in close proximity to the city.

Transformations on the Ground

The team faced a lot of backlash from other regional media which had business or political affiliations. At first, locals questioned whether Free Radio was truly free. However, as the newsroom stuck to journalistic standards and monitored local developments in an objective way, it attracted a greater audience. Listeners in occupied territories tuned in to Free Radio, too, despite it being blocked by Russian authorities; they also began requesting more news about Donetsk and other areas under Russian control. This happened years before the big war of 2022.

"A lot of pro-Ukrainian people reached out to us from the occupied areas," Anastasiia said, "Many recommended us to those who were not necessarily pro-Ukrainian, but who wanted to get credible news. We position ourselves as a Ukrainian media with a pro-Ukrainian stance, but we follow journalistic standards, so our audience had nothing to complain about in terms of reporting."

The journalist believes that access to an independent news source helped locals question Kremlin narratives in an area where pro-Russian sentiments have been very strong. Proximity and family ties in Russia made this border area susceptible to Russian propaganda, and few local media dared to challenge that.

"A lot of people started to reflect and analyze what Russia truly was after they got our content," Anastasiia went on, "I have examples of young students from the occupied territories, who, thanks to these reflections, chose to leave and seek higher education in Ukraine-controlled areas."

People in Bakhmut, too, liked the idea of having an independent media platform that focused on local issues and that held elected officials accountable.

"We realized that our idea is working when our stories contributed to better decision-making on the ground," Anastasiia said, "For example, we analyzed how accessible the voting polls were, and this enabled more wheelchair users to vote."

The team investigated cases of corruption, such as murky public procurement or meddling in elections, and the newsroom also reported on the Russian troops amassing close to the Ukrainian border in early 2022, thus warning locals of a potential full-scale invasion.

Displacement and Destruction

Free Radio's newsroom was well prepared when Russia launched its full-scale war against Ukraine on February 24.

"We watched carefully what Russia was doing, and we knew something big was coming," Anastasiia recalled.

Still, the team did not think that the invasion would be this huge or that the Russians would try to take Kyiv. The expectation was that the Russian army would rather try to capture the rest of Donbas as they already controlled chunks of this region since 2014.

By the time Russian missiles started falling across Ukraine, Free Radio's team had already shipped off most of its equipment to other parts of the country. Some team members evacuated from Bakhmut right away while others chose to remain and continued reporting from the city.

By 2023, however, the entire team had fled. Most of the city is gone, anyway.

"Our community is displaced, and so are we," Anastasiia reflected, "It is hard to remain a local media because our audience is stranded all over Ukraine and Europe. Their needs and interests have changed, but they still care about their hometown, and they want to know what's going on there, what happened to their houses, and what the local officials are doing."

Right now, the team covers evacuations and helps Bakhmut locals navigate the new reality of displacement and destruction of their homes. Journalists encourage those who remain in the city to leave; and help them understand how to get help in a new place once they flee from danger.

"The last time I went to Bakhmut was in the end of 2022," Anastasiia recalled, "We reported from the frontlines, and we did a few other trips close to the fighting areas. However, Russians destroyed one of our TV towers, so we are somewhat limited in how many people in the area we can reach. It's heartbreaking to lose this close connection with your audience, but we're trying to serve their needs from across Ukraine."

While the team is working hard to survive in this new environment, it is already making plans.

"We want to be one of the first media to return after liberation," Anastasiia said, "We want to be the watchdogs tracking down renovation spending and to scale this up across the area. We want to monitor the local governments and expand to the entire Donetsk region."

The journalist is hopeful that the reintegration of the occupied areas will come soon, and her team is already prepping for that. The journalist plans to continue the local work after the victory and cover the issues national or international media overlook.

"We want to be one of the best local media on the local market," Anastasiia said.

"We saw the impact our reporting had, and we know that these transformations cannot be reversed," she concluded proudly, "Objectively, we went beyond our expectations because we did not only create an alternative to pro-Russian oligarch-owned media but became the one media organization people used for analysis and explanations."

Death by Water

The Nova Kakhovka Dam Explosion May Become the Biggest Environmental Catastrophe in Europe in Decades

June 2023

"In the morning, the water stream was crazy," Tania Kniazeva said, "The flow carried everything: there were mines and military equipment."

"In an hour, I saw that the water level increased by 40 centimeters," she added.

Tania is a resident of Kherson, a city with 300,000 residents in the South of Ukraine. Located right next to Ukraine's biggest river, Dnipro, it is only 50 kilometers away from the Kakhovka dam, which exploded on Tuesday. Ukraine blames Russia, and Russia blames Ukraine for the attack, and to date, the culprit has not been verified. According to experts, an internal blast is likely to have caused the destruction of the Russian-controlled dam.

"The river is growing larger and larger," Tania continued, "I've seen houses going under, and I can only imagine what's happening on the lower left bank of Dnipro."

"In Kherson, we've got some safe places still, but many people are coming here after fleeing from the lower areas," the woman added, "I know that in the occupied areas, it is much worse, and people are sitting on the roofs because Russians didn't evacuate people."

Nova Kakhovka dam holds back a major reservoir in Southern Ukraine. It has been under Russian occupation for more than a year. Already in October last year, Ukraine's President Volodymyr Zelenskyy warned that Russians were planning to blow up the dam, endangering hundreds of thousands of Ukrainians in the area, not to mention other risks.

In November 2022, Ukraine liberated Kherson and other nearby areas on the right bank of Dnipro. The dam, however, and other parts of the region on the left bank remained under Russian control. The left bank is lower than the right one, so while the dam's destruction will affect Ukrainians on both sides of the river, the ones under occupation are going to suffer much more.

Tuesday Morning

Tania's house in Kherson is relatively close to the waterfront, and from her home, she could easily spot the unusual stream that started on Tuesday morning. Around 6 o'clock, many locals began getting messages that the Nova Kakhovka dam was blown up. The information started spreading through Telegram channels and messengers, and people from Ukraine-controlled areas could communicate with those in Russia-occupied territories.

"It was so bizarre to look at the water in the morning and see that powerful flow," Tania recalled, "A lot of Russian equipment was flowing through the stream while Russians were still trying to shoot at the city. Basically, they knew that people would be evacuated, so they kept on targeting Kherson to prevent locals from leaving the endangered areas."

At first, some people didn't realize what was happening; many refused to leave.

"When the water started coming, some neighbors thought it would stop quickly, and it would not reach the houses and residential areas," Tania explained, "But in a few hours, we realized that we had to go because the water kept on coming."

"I saw lots of wild animals trying to get to safety as they were roaming around the streets of my city," she added, "They ran from the nearby areas that were already under the water and were moving together with people to places that were still dry."

By Wednesday morning, three entire districts of this large city were already completely underwater. Many of the 300,000 residents had to flee to other parts of Ukraine because their houses were gone.

"Luckily, I got a boat, and I could navigate," Tania said, "My house is still okay, too, so I was not as bad as others. I helped evacuate some animals and people in the areas where it was still possible to get in. But there are areas where the stream is really strong and where it's impossible to get in."

"So many people, elderly and immobile, are probably dead because of this crime," she continued.

"And the water is really cold, too," the woman added.

The Dam

The reservoir at the base of Nova Kakhovka dam is roughly the same size as the Great Salt Lake in Utah and half the size of the EU's biggest lake, Vanern. In the past, it provided water for large areas in Southern Ukraine. The reservoir was also a main source of water for Russian-occupied Crimea. When Russians annexed the peninsula in 2014, Ukraine blocked the channel linking water from Nova Kakhovka, and Crimea suffered a water crisis. Occupying the dam in 2022 was a strategic move for the Russians.

Thanks to the dam, Ukraine also maintained a hydroelectric station in the area, which contributed about 2% of Ukraine's electricity usage, so the damage is expected to come mostly from the destructive flooding, though it may have minor implications on Ukraine's energy infrastructure that has already been badly damaged by Russian missiles.

Because the reservoir was a key source for cooling the Zaporizhzhia nuclear plant—located nearby and also under Russian occupation—the explosion sparked fears of nuclear dangers associated with the attack. There are several backup water supplies that can be used, meaning that the risk of catastrophe has been averted for now, but IAEA Director General Grossi said in a statement, "This is making an already very difficult and unpredictable nuclear safety and security situation even more so."

The dam's destruction has affected at least 300,000 people living on the right and left banks of Dnipro—residents of Kherson, the biggest city in the area, as well as smaller towns and villages. Some are already under water such as the village of Oleshky in the Russian-occupied territories, some 20 kilometers from Kherson. Ukrainian government cannot access these territories to help with evacuations due to Russia's control. In Ukraine-controlled areas, the evacuations were complicated by constant shooting from the Russian side.

"They were targeting us when people were fleeing," Tania said, "They knew that civilians are trying to get to safety, so they launched massive mortar strikes. So, you can imagine — people had to escape both the water and the Russian fire." According to Tania, Russian mines and other military tools were carried in by the water stream, endangering the situation in the city. And she worries that these mines could detonate.

Occupied Areas

"A bunch of villages in the Oleshky district are badly affected," said Yevhen Ryshchyk, Oleshky's mayor. Oleshky is a small town near Kherson under Russian occupation. While Yevhen could escape and now lives in the Ukraine-controlled part of the Kherson region, he keeps in touch with locals remaining in Oleshky and nearby villages. "I received reports from locals that parts of the villages went underwater in a matter of hours," he said, "We cannot help people there, and we keep getting reports that the town of Oleshky is getting underwater, too. The newest update is that the water level increased by at least three feet."

The mayor warned that there is an increased risk of infectious diseases as a result of the floods, and there is an expectation that the water levels will increase even more in a few days. The water level is projected to peak in the 3 to 5 days following the dam's explosion.

"In the beginning, locals hoped that Russians would evacuate them," the mayor said, "There were some unconfirmed reports that so-called authorities would provide boats or buses to get the people out. However, as the mayor stressed, this did not happen. "Russians left people on their own," the mayor continued, "There are no boats, and there is still a curfew in the occupied areas. Those who tried to evacuate on their own were prohibited from leaving the area. This is genocide."

There are reports and drone videos of Ukrainians stuck on their rooftops in the occupied areas, unable to leave — with no help on the way. There is no information on how many people are dead or missing in the Russian-controlled areas as a result of the catastrophe; the World Data Center projects that the left bank will be 8 times more affected than the right bank.

Humans are not the only ones affected. Many animals have drowned because of the floods. In Russian-occupied Nova Kakhovka, nearly 300 zoo animals were killed. The Russian administration didn't allow staff to release the animals, so most of them died in their cages. Only birds—ducks and swans—survived.

The dam's destruction is going to affect at least 80 towns, cities, and villages, and its impact on Ukraine's ecosystem is hard to overestimate—it has already been referred to by Ukrainian President Zelenskyy as one of the biggest environmental disasters of the era, and the UN's Secretary-General António Guterres has labeled it a "monumental humanitarian, economic and ecological catastrophe."

In addition to the damage to people's homes, the damage done to the ecosystem—including natural resorts and fertile soil—may be irreversible, according to Ukrainian environmentalists, and carry all of the characteristics of ecocide. According to the environmentalist Lyudmyla Tzyhanok, the dam's explosion will lead to the transformation of the entire ecosystem of the region. In addition to impacts on drinking water in the area, the dam's destruction will lead to the death of a huge number of fish, waterlogging of drained lands, and up to 1.5 million climate refugees from the affected areas.

"We're going to get a new desert..." she said in an interview with Voice of America, "And this will lead to field storms, rising temperatures in the region, and a drought risk."

Dismantling Russian Imperialism One Step at a Time

Ukrainians Are Coming to Terms with the Legacy of Colonization

June 2023

"Decolonization does not have a clear start or an end," said Mariam, "For it to happen, we first must come to terms with our own history and suffering that comes with it."

"Unfortunately, there is no algorithm we can just follow," she added, "No decolonization process is the same, and it is especially tricky for Ukraine as a former white colony."

Mariam Naiem is a cultural researcher. Throughout her work, she is educating the world about Ukraine through the post-colonial lens. A Ukrainian of Afghan origin, Mariam tries to shed light on cultural aspects of the Russian war and decolonize discourse about Ukraine.

Mariam spoke of decolonization long before the concept became well-known among Ukrainians. While experts and intellectuals spoke of Russian imperialism toward Ukraine for a long time, it was only after 2014, and, most notably, with 2022 Russia's war, that decolonization became a mainstream topic for reflection in Ukraine's society.

Even now, the concept remains difficult.

"The process of decolonization is subjective," Mariam said, "It has no algorithms, so we need to analyze what elements work better for Ukrainian society around the decolonial discourse. And then, we need to learn how to communicate this to foreigners."

For the first time in the country's recent history, Ukrainians get a chance not only to explain their history to the world but also to get people to listen. Prior to the 2022 Russian war, there was little interest in Ukraine globally, and the few news that did appear was mostly shaped by pro-Russian and imperialist narratives. Now, there are many voices like Mariam's which are working on bringing Ukrainian perspectives forward; and these voices are getting more recognition.

Understanding the Legacy of Empire

"The idea that Ukraine is a post-colonial nation existed among scientists for a long time," Mariam said, "However, it was often ignored by the general public or international audiences. It was in 2022 that a need arose to explain very concretely why Russia invaded Ukraine."

As the experts explained, the Russian full-scale invasion was the catalyst for this renewed understanding. The war had no political or economic sense, and it carried out few benefits for Russians; that was the reason many Ukrainians refused to believe in its imminence. However, the war made perfect sense from the imperialist prism.

"For Russians, it would be much more logical to continue living with annexed Crimea and promote narratives about "Russia's greatness," Mariam explained, "Starting a big war was illogical in this case, but if you add Russian imperialism to the equation, everything becomes clear."

"That is why when we speak of decolonization, we understand that Russia is not an [former] empire, but it remains an empire," she added, "It continues its imperial existence and perceives Ukraine as a colony."

In Mariam's opinion, Ukraine remained Russia's colony for much longer than many realized. It was first colonized by the Russian Empire in the mid-17th century and then continued to be a colony of the USSR, similar to other Soviet republics. What's more, given the many interventions of the Russian state in Ukraine's affairs, such as financing pro-Russian politicians and launching economic warfare against Ukraine's pro-European leadership in the mid-2000s, Ukraine acted as Russia's neo-colony in the modern period all the way until 2014. Then, in 2014, Ukrainians organized the Revolution of Dignity, which, in many ways, manifested their desire to break away from Russia and its influence.

Colonialism in the Modern Era

"There is imperialism, and there is neo-imperialism or neo-colonialism," Mariam explained, "Colonialism, simply put, is when I go to your house with cops and demand you to let me live in there; otherwise, I will kill you. But, if I bribe your landlords, and they, without you knowing, give me all your house resources, then we're talking about neo-colonialism. This is when one country bribes or manipulates the political elites of another country and this way, another country lives for the benefit of the empire. Empires do not wish their colonies to develop independent political elites, so they destroy them."

Given Russia's continuous presence in Ukraine's information space and its regular meddling in domestic affairs – such as the economic wars in the early 2000s, the presence of the Russian military in Crimea, and the financing of pro-Russian politicians – the Ukrainian society was strongly influenced by pro-Russian narratives and often supported policies and decisionmakers acting against Ukraine's interests that rather benefitted Russia. For example, society was split over its desire to join the EU and NATO due to pro-Russian narratives that painted the West negatively.

This also explains why talking about decolonization and Russia's imperial legacy was not part of Ukraine's education curriculum and why so many Ukrainians are only starting to address these issues now when this legacy is more pronounced than ever.

"Decolonization has two dimensions," Mariam said, "The first come is institutional and state-driven, and the other one is personal. Without the state implementing decolonization policies, this process is extremely slow."

Whitewashing Russian Colonialism

In Russia, the imperial legacy is celebrated and promoted, and Russia's state TV continually streams praise for Russia's imperial legacy. Russia also lobbies for the legitimacy of its territorial claims toward its former colonies on the international stage, such as misappropriating Ukrainian artists as Russian and advertising imperialism through beauty pageants like Miss Universe.

This contrasts sharply with the way colonialism is approached in many former European empires, where the past is viewed from a critical lens. "Russian colonialism receives less criticism than, for example, British, and there are many reasons for that," Mariam explained, "There is a post-colonial theory which is often linked with Marxism. As a lot of intellectuals working on post-colonial theory were, in some ways, Marxists, they had sympathies toward the Soviet Union. The USSR, in its propaganda, very clearly emphasized that they were an anti-colonial entity."

"What's more, when we analyze the definition of Russian imperialism, the first person who started using it was Vladimir Lenin," the expert added, "Lenin applied the term in Ukraine's context, stating that 'we need to help get rid of Russian imperialism.' With this, he aimed to gain the trust of Ukrainian political elites so they would support Communists. Many intellectuals believed that the USSR was anti-imperialist."

In addition, there is a greater historical context. As the USSR existed alongside fascism and Nazism, Soviet propaganda was very active in whitewashing itself as anti-colonial — despite having all the features of an empire. Thus, former Soviet republics which managed to regain independence in the nineties should be referred to as post-colonial states, as Mariam put it.

Atypical Colonies

A big emphasis of Russian propaganda is claiming that Ukrainians are Russians and that Ukraine belongs to Russia. This false statement has been picked up by many Western intellectuals to justify Russia's war and reject the evidence of Russian imperialism.

"One of the reasons that some Western scientists don't perceive Ukraine as a colony is due to the 'overseas theory,' which implies that a colony must be far away from the imperial center, ideally separated by water," Mariam explained.

In addition, colonialist discourse often frames colonies as territories with non-white populations. "There are political scientists who think that white-majority colonies do not exist," Mariam said, "In this context, Ukraine stands out because it's close to Russia geographically, and the majority of Ukrainians are white. This is a problem because Russia is different from many other empires. For example, when the UK colonized India, they did not claim that Indians were British. Russia instead simply devours countries next to it, and this way, it expands the notion of itself."

"In this context, Ukraine or Belarus do not have many differentiating factors from Russia besides language," the expert continued, "We look similar, we are majority Christian Orthodox, and we are close geographically. So, language is the main demarcation sign between us and the empire. Language is vital for this separation."

Russification, a policy of replacing local languages with Russian, was aimed at exactly that: destroying the unique languages which separated the empire from its colonies. Russification lasted for centuries and continued in independent Ukraine due to Russian interference in Ukraine. It started being addressed only after the Revolution of Dignity in 2014, which profoundly changed Ukrainian society.

Decolonial Catharsis

"The Revolution of Dignity was a decolonial catharsis moment for Ukraine," Mariam explained, "The revolution was about separating ourselves from Russian imperialism. It was the moment when we decided that we did not want to live like before anymore."

Decolonial catharsis marks a moment when the colonized choose to break with the colonizers, and it often happens thanks to the presence of new independent political elites. In 2014, Ukrainians still lacked such political leaders, so the Revolution of Dignity — a mass movement that ousted the pro-Russian government from power — was carried out by society as a whole and not specific parties or decision-makers.

"Even without widely accepted political elites, Ukrainians were so willing to get out of the empire that they created a revolution," Mariam stressed, "It's very hard to do without the leaders, and this is a proud moment for Ukrainian society, which is one of the reasons not to feel as a victim. The unity of Ukrainian society back then surprised me, and it keeps on surprising me as it still lasts."

Revisiting History

Ukraine shares similar experiences with other countries colonized by Russia, such as former Soviet republics. As Mariam suggested, all these nations can work together as they have evidence that both modern Russia and its previous forms—such as the USSR—are imperial entities. "This will give us a notion that we are not alone in this, and we're all working toward decolonization," she added.

The first step, however, is domestic. As Mariam put it, before talking about its colonial past to the world, Ukrainians need to understand their history first. For example, Ukraine still lacks a systematic discussion on its collective trauma; and decolonization discourse is missing from education programs in schools or unis.

"We cannot change history, but we can change our attitude toward it," she proceeded, "Yes, we were a colony of the USSR, but it does not change that we always had Ukrainian artists and scientists, and this led to cultural developments to some extent. It is necessary to analyze what we gained in culture despite the oppression of the Soviet Union and what we developed despite all these obstacles. We need to analyze what we gained from this experience, and not only lost."

"The most important thing is to include decolonization concept into our school curriculum," Mariam highlighted, "Without a change in culture and education institutions, we will keep repeating the same mistakes. We need to build a new Ukraine with new symbols and a new understanding of history, which will be more Ukrainian and not post-Soviet. For this, we need cultural experts and historians to create a new cultural policy that would also be included in our education."

Some of the existing decolonization policies include language-related laws aimed at protecting the Ukrainian language, which has been discriminated against for centuries. Other examples include creating special quotas for Ukrainian musicians on radio stations;

and revisiting the history of Holodomor, a Soviet-led genocide of Ukrainians, and other traumatic parts of history.

As the expert put it, it is not easy to accept one's past as a colony; there is a lot of stigma around it.

"We need to admit that we were a colony without trying to hide or whitewash history somehow," she added, "It is painful to understand that we were taken advantage of for centuries. It is hard, but it is important for our understanding."

"The idea of colonization has been kept in the dark for a long time," Mariam concluded, "The most vital thing for us is to educate our children about it."

For Mariam, imperialism is like a disease, and educating youth about it is like giving them a vaccine to fight off this illness.

"We Carry On, but It Doesn't Mean We're Not in Pain"

A Ukrainian Psychologist Speaks on Resilience and Trauma amid Russian War

July 2023

"The fact that you and I are talking right now means we carry on," Olha said, "We adapt. It does not mean we're not in pain, or that it's not difficult or scary. But we go on."

Olha Kukharuk is a psychologist. She's been working with war-affected people since 2015, a year after Russia launched a smaller-scale war in Eastern Ukraine. Back then, the conflict received much less attention, and those directly affected — both soldiers and displaced civilians — often struggled with their traumatic experiences in silence.

In 2022, Russia expanded its war, and Ukraine's entire population was directly impacted. This meant more work for professionals like Olha, who continued her psychological support groups while also being affected by the war.

"If you're Ukrainian, you have war experience regardless where you are," Olha explained, "Even if you're away, you may have someone on the frontline or under occupation, so you worry for them. We all have a collection of different war experiences that we live through, and they are complex and hard. Those are not the experiences you would want to have in your life, and we manage them with tears, anger, and despair."

"War experience is a mix of emotions," she added, "Some of them may be even good such as finding relief or using black humor, which is typical for Ukrainians. The key thing is our resilience, or the ability to live through this, and renew ourselves afterwards."

Mental Care Systems, Stigma, and Trauma

"I have been working in the field of crisis psychology since 2015," Olha recalled, "This is when I started working with Ukrainian servicemen fighting in the war in Donbas."

Olha has years of experience in psychology. Always interested in the way people lived in society, she worked at the Institute of Social and Political Psychology in Kyiv when Russia occupied parts of Eastern Ukraine in 2014.

"When the Donbas war began, I started volunteering," the expert said, "At first, it was general volunteering, not related to my field. Later, I started paying attention to my colleagues who focused on psychological support. I realized that it was a very necessary work which I could do given my background, and this is how a second stage of my professional life began. I started working with servicemen, then with veterans, and then I continued with rehabilitation, social psychology, trauma experience, and so on."

Prior to 2022, Ukraine was developing a better response system to handle the influx of veterans and other war-affected people from the East. Then, the full-scale invasion happened.

"Nobody expected such a big wave of people suffering from mental health problems linked to the war," Olha continued, "So there is a huge human resources' gap that the system cannot cover. In a regular hospital, there may be three psychologists for 200 or 300 patients. We also don't have long-term rehabilitations for people; they normally last around 2-3 weeks, and there is a need to make them as efficient as possible."

On a national level, the state is implementing a Mental Health Gap program which trains regular doctors to recognize war-linked mental issues and redirect patients to specialized hospitals.

For the military, there are psychology-focused institutions, too. Yet, even there, there may be challenges finding enough staff.

"To put it simply — yes, we do need psychological rehabilitation, but even if you're put in a hospital, you won't necessarily be able to get it," Olha explained, "There is a lack of a systematic approach. It's somewhat similar to how Ukraine gets arms from the rest of the world — there are many issues on different levels, and civil society steps in when institutions don't work. You can call it a "Ukrainian approach."

For instance, many local NGOs are filling the gaps where the state does not have the capacity to do so — they are organizing support groups, launching mental health initiatives, and raising funds for physical and psychological rehabilitation of veterans and civilians. The fundraising is tricky, as big donors don't normally want to support anything that directly benefits active servicemen.

Besides, the work of NGOs cannot replace the system, and as Olha points out, the Ukrainian government will eventually need to expand its focus and financing of rehabilitation-related programs.

"But for now, what should we do in this situation?" Olha reflected, "Well, to fight as we're already fighting. We cannot exaggerate the importance of psychological rehabilitation. We need to develop the system, and we need to help people seeking aid."

Ukrainian Resilience

"In a classic point of view, resilience is your ability to restore yourself," Olha explained, "It is your fullness. It means that you don't have to have a post-traumatic stress syndrome if you experienced a traumatic experience; or even if you get it, you're able to overcome it."

"When it comes to Ukrainian resilience, we're talking about strategies to survive and renew oneself not only physically, but mentally," she continued, "Ukrainians have a set of strategies to carry on with all of the different experiences they have, and they do it either individually or collectively."

As Olha highlights, understanding Ukrainian resilience may be difficult, especially for non-Ukrainians. Often, Ukraine is presented through one of the two extremes. On one hand, many foreigners imagine a trauma-affected Ukrainian, full of tears and pain, who complains about the war. That is why many foreigners are shocked to meet Ukrainians who do not conform to these stereotypes, or when they see videos of Ukrainian cities bustling with life, and people , trying to carry on amid war.

"Ukrainians get comments from abroad like: "How come you're sitting in McDonalds if there is war in your country?" Olha said, "Or 'Why are Ukrainians drinking coffee if they should be sad?'"

Another extreme is portraying Ukrainians as unbreakable, and exaggerating their resilience.

"The truth is, we are somewhat in-between these two extremes," Olha explained, "As long as we're affected but not defeated by the war, we are able to manage. A lot of people who experience huge losses can carry on thanks to courage, anger, and faith in victory. Our faith in freedom and justice also helps us. People are in a lot of pain, but they manage to balance this out by their need to live. You may hear explosions at night, but you wake up in the morning and go to work. You adapt."

As Olha stresses, Ukrainian resilience does not mean that people simply ignore the war — but rather, they invent mechanisms that help them cope with this dramatic reality. The trauma is already leaving a mark on many Ukrainians, and its impact is going to increase over time. However, the psychologist highlights, most Ukrainians manage to resist it.

"This experience is hard to communicate abroad," Olha reflected, "We need to explain that this is our new normal, and we learned how to live in this reality even though it may be difficult and scary. We need to emphasize that this is our home, so it is important to stay here and carry on with living. While we adapted to many things, it does not mean that this is not frightening. It does not mean we're not in pain."

"There is a Ukrainian joke that summarizes this," she continued, "A patient has a knife stuck in his back. A doctor asks: 'Are you in pain?' 'Only when I am laughing,' the patient replies. This is about Ukrainians now."

Fatigue and Beyond

"The longer we stay in the war, the more we feel exhausted," Olha says, "Social connections are becoming more and more important in this case."

To deal with growing war fatigue, people seek social support, the expert continues, and there is still a lot of it among Ukrainians. She shares her own example: when her home area was hit with missiles, the community responded immediately. On the next day after the attack, locals affected by the strike were already receiving help from strangers online and offline.

"People helping people becomes an automatic process," Olha said, "Volunteers are still going strong, and locals remain engaged. However, we are less likely to notice this help as the war goes on. There is a paradox: the more we need support, the less we notice it, and the more we pay attention to negative things."

People become more vulnerable to bad news or harmful comments the longer they are affected by the war environment — especially if their experiences differ. For example, a refugee may feel that Ukrainians who chose to remain inside the country are judgmental of their decision, or the other way around. War fatigue and long-term exhaustion increase the risk of social conflicts. Locally, there are mediators and facilitators working with internally displaced people and other social groups — but they cannot cover everyone affected.

"We will pay a high price for this emotional exhaustion," Olha signed, "That is why I organize webinars on resilience. There, I highlight the necessity to rely on your functionality and notice your achievements. When we're traumatized, we focus on things we cannot control. Instead, we need to think of our values to see why we're doing what we're doing."

"We're fighting for the sake of our families, future, and country," she added, "These values support us immensely, and they give us power to go on. When you stand on your values, you have a strong foundation, so the same burden is much easier to lift when you know what you believe in."

"This War Is a Way to Relive and Reflect on Historical Experiences"

Ukraine experienced a major unity moment when the full-scale war started. The country's residents shared fears and confusion, but also their resolution.

"The more vulnerable we are, the more we care about our values," Olha explained, "We care about Ukrainian language if we speak it; we care about our home whenever there is a risk of losing it."

Language conflicts are a good example: Ukrainian speakers feel threatened when they hear Russian on the streets of their cities because they are used to marking this space as their own. It is normal for them to hear Ukrainian outside, which represents security for them. For native Russian speakers, which represent about one sixth of Ukrainians, sticking to their native language means preserving their identity. Thus, language can lead to conflicts—but also to social transformations.

"Russian speakers are going through an identity change," Olha reflected, "It's hard because it means they need to reflect on Russia, on many myths from their youth, and on different values. It is difficult to separate your childhood lullabies from Russia. Most people understand that they have to do it, but it is very subjective. I feel bad for these people because it is a hard path for changes, and we need to highlight the fantastic work they did with themselves by saying no to what they used to love. They are rebuilding their foundations."

The war creates a new space for reliving—and rethinking historical trauma, too. Besides language transformations, many Ukrainians are reflecting how years of colonialism and oppression affect them and their families.

"Those things have an impact because they are a part of our history, our worldview," Olha explained, "It is interesting to see how a lot of Ukrainians are now identifying as true fighters against fascism given that Russia acts as a fascist state. Further, we need to reflect on our post-colonial mentality from the Soviet times because it's also part of the trauma."

For example, during Holodomor Remembrance Day, people shared photos of candles next to a gun saying "Never again." Holodomor, or the Great Famine, was a genocide of Ukrainians carried out by the Soviets during 1930s. Similarly, when Russians blew up the Kakhovka dam, a lot of ruins of old churches and ancient fortresses were discovered under the water. This spurred many discussions in Ukraine on historical parallels and reliving trauma from Russian aggression.

Reconciliation as a Defense Mechanism

"Foreigners recognize what Ukraine is, but they do not know much besides stereotypes of Ukrainian victims of Ukrainian heroes," Olha said, "They do not know historical context of Russia's war of aggression."

As experts puts it, people associate the war with victimhood, but they have a hard time understanding other feelings Ukrainians share.

"I recently traveled to Ireland to talk about my work in Ukraine," Olha continued, "On the same day, there was a big missile attack near my home while my son was there. So I spent a lot of time on the phone with my child and still did my presentation. It was not a good experience, but it showed that I could continue my work while carrying that inside me. This shocks foreigners."

This explains why many peace plans — which tend to overlook Ukrainians and their war experiences — stem from abroad. The same goes for Western-driven reconciliation attempts for Ukrainians and Russians, which receive a lot of criticism in Ukraine.

"Reconciliation is a defense mechanism for Westerners," Olha said, "They think that if they force Ukrainians to reconcile with Russia, they won't need to read shocking news from Ukraine anymore. A lot of Westerners still think of Russia as a great nation with a great culture, so it's hard for them to accept the fact that it is not just Putin. This forced reconciliation is a defense tool for finding solutions."

"Reconciliation meddling also allows many Westerns to increase their own importance," the expert concluded, "There are Ukrainians coming into their countries disrupting their comfort and telling them to stop business with Russian partners. These Westerners are expected to change their worldviews and make some efforts. Many choose an easy path instead: "Let's make them reconcile!" This comes up when people lack context about Russia and Ukraine."

The Struggle of the Black Sea amid Russian War

The Environmentalists Are Assessing the Damage Done to the Sea after Kakhovka Dam Explosion

July 2023

"The Black Sea has always been vulnerable, more so because of the war," says Olena Marushevska, an environmental expert at the National Marine Hub Ukraine. "So it will take Ukraine a lot of time and resources to restore its waters after the victory."

"We're already starting to assess the damage done by the Russians in the last year and half," she adds, "It is difficult to put a price on the loss of biodiversity or dolphins killed, but we've got economic and legal instruments for that. The bottom line is that we'll need to do a thorough analysis of all the war impacts to bring the sea back to normal."

Originally from Kyiv, Olena Marushevska now spends half her time in Odesa, Ukraine's largest port city, where she works on environmental and educational projects. Prior to Russia's full-scale invasion of Ukraine, Olena's work included research and outreach events on biodiversity and sea protection. Now, her team is focusing on war-related issues such as mining safety — and understanding the impact of military-induced pollution on the coastal waters.

"The Russian war has had a negative impact on the Black Sea on many different levels," Olena explains. "We have not been able to do a full screening of its waters yet due to the war, but once it's over, we plan to do a large international expedition on that. This will help determine how we can get rid of the marine pollution and waste and what to do with the trash that we cannot get rid of — such as Russia's battleship Moscow which sunk a year ago."

"Plus, we're already seeing the long-term impacts of the Kakhovka dam explosion," she adds. "While there are some consequences that we can address now, there are bigger issues that are

179

difficult to solve—such as removing all the mines that got into the Black Sea after the catastrophe."

Pre-war struggles

The Black Sea stands out from other European seas because it is semi-closed. It has only a small connection with the Mediterranean and Aegean seas via the Turkish Straits and the tiny Sea of Mamara, which means that most of the pollution that goes into the Black Sea stays there.

"The sea also receives water from many large rivers such as the Dnipro and the Danube, which used to be considered 'a sewage system' for the entirety of Europe," Olena says. "So, the discharge of large rivers is a lot for this relatively small sea. It is very vulnerable in comparison to other seas—given that it depends on the water quality from many rivers."

There are positives in these characteristics, however—such as richer biodiversity due to the mixture of freshwater and salt water.

"Even in ancient times, the Greeks used to fish on the Black Sea because they considered it to be richer in fish and tastier than the Mediterranean or Aegean," Olena smiles. "This is also because the Black Sea is less salty in comparison to other seas."

The sea is shared by six countries: Ukraine, Romania, Bulgaria, Turkey, Georgia, and Russia. While the pollution levels are similar across different coasts, the shelf area—which is shallower—tends to be more polluted. This covers Ukrainian and Romanian parts.

From 2016 to 2019, Ukraine and the EU implemented the 'Improving Environmental Monitoring in the Black Sea' project. The latter classified the waters according to their environmental status and pollution levels, with blue and green as clean and almost clean, and yellow, orange, and red as those with higher levels of pollution.

"Near Odesa, we had a lot of yellow because there was not enough wastewater treatment and marine litter management," Olena explains. "It was also yellow and orange where Danube enters the Black Sea. In addition, we classified 124 priority substances in the sea water, but back then, it was pharmaceuticals, pesticides, and plasticisers, and others. There were no war-related substances.

I think if we were to do this analysis again, we'd find a lot of missile fuel-related substances, and so on. So, after the victory, we'd need to do a broad analysis of the Black Sea to see what new polluting substances should be added to the list."

The Black Sea is also the only one that is linked with the Sea of Azov, a much smaller and shallower sea in the South of Ukraine. Pre-war, it used to be a sanctuary for dolphins, but it's been under Russian occupation since March 2022.

"We know that the wastewater infrastructure is completely destroyed there, so all the trash and sewage go directly into the sea," Olena says. "It is even more vulnerable than the Black Sea, and it carries its pollution there, too."

War and its consequences

When the Russians blew up the Kakhovka dam in June, they only made the matters worse. Primarily, the huge water wave after the explosion brought in a large quantity of waste. It covers the sea surface, which prevents a lot of species from living there.

"Another problem is that we have an increased risk of mine explosions," Olena stresses. "There are lots of sea mines, anti-tank mines, and so on, which were brought into the sea when the dam blew up. Over time, these mines will get harder to detect and remove, so we don't know how to solve this problem for now."

Besides, the sea suffered a huge influx of chemical and organic waste, and is now covered in phytoplankton blooms that change the water's color—unusual for early summer. Plus, there is a lot of toxic algae, which has another negative impact on sea inhabitants.

Many coastal areas have also been badly damaged—such as the Kinburn Spit, in Mykolaiv Oblast, which used to be a sanctuary for many birds, and which is of international importance under the Ramsar Convention for wetland conservation. It was burned in a 4,000 hectare wildfire caused by rockets and then mined by Russia. Restoring these areas is difficult if not impossible given the impact that the war has had on them.

"The good thing about the Black Sea is that it is not fully in a state of war, so fish and dolphins can escape from our territory and come back when the war is over," Olena explains. "For example, Georgian and Romanian coasts now have many more dolphins than before. I hope that when the war is over, these species will return."

Thinking of recovery

Saving the Black Sea will be a step-by-step process — and it will have to be implemented alongside Ukraine's general reconstruction.

"Think of it like a doctor's visit," Olena explains. "First the medic gives you a diagnosis and some meds. After you take them, the doctor inspects you again to see what's working in this treatment, and what doesn't. Sea analysis will be somewhat similar. There will be a preliminary screening, which will lead to a development of a five-year-long program to improve the quality of the Black Sea. Afterwards, there will be another big monitoring mission which will analyze the implementation and introduce new solutions for new problems."

The fact that Ukraine is an EU candidate country can help it in restoration of the Black Sea. The EU demands that every country implements its Marine Strategy Framework Directive, which will require Ukraine to analyze and classify the sea in different colors according to its environmental status and pollution levels, and come up with an action plan for every area of the sea that is yellow, orange, or red. Ukraine's Reconstruction Plan already includes various measures that are related to the sea restoration, including construction of wastewater treatment facilities.

"We have a unique chance to restore our sea based on innovative practices," Olena highlights. "Replacing wastewater infrastructure is expensive and time-consuming. However, now that it is gone, we must install a new one that meets the EU requirements. So, the sea would be treated in a better and more innovative way according to the EU directives."

The same applies to sea-related human activity — such as fishing or tourism — which would require more sustainable policymaking to reduce waste, for instance. In addition, Ukraine would need to analyze new polluting substances that may have appeared in the sea after the war — and whose characteristics are yet unknown. Furthermore, the assessing and analysis part would have to take place together with the EU — which would simplify the process of getting the funds for renovation.

"We have to do all reconstruction together, like working on sea pollution and general pollution reduction at the same time," Olena says. "This process has to be all-inclusive, and it will need to include our international partners to make it as efficient and sustainable as possible."

"One year after the victory, we'll be able to see the first results, such as the return of disturbed sea creatures," she concludes. "Those sea refugees will come back — just like the people who had to escape because of the war. This is the first step. The second step — full renovation — will take longer."

"I Never Wanted to Join the Army, but Then, Russia Invaded Us."

A Senior Combat Medic Talks of Her Life and Work on the Frontline in Ukraine.

July 2023

"Two weeks before the invasion I realized that something might happen," Alina Sarnatska said matter of factly. "So I went to the Red Cross and did a training with them on medical aid," she added. "I got their certificate. Then I went to apply to be a medic in the army. They rejected me."

But Alina did join Ukraine's Armed Forces, even though it was on her second try, and thanks to an acquaintance. Now, she serves as a senior combat medic of an infantry squadron. Her location is Eastern Ukraine, the frontline.

"I never planned to go to the army," Alina sighed. "I would have never done it if it wasn't for the war. But there is no choice."

"Russia invaded us," she added. "You can check on the map what it looks like in comparison to Ukraine. So it's a very difficult war, and there is nothing good about it."

"Are You Afraid of Blood?"

"Before the war, I used to research human rights," Alina said. "I worked on different projects against domestic violence and consulting on methods to prevent it."

"But you see, when a foreign army comes, kills, rapes, and organizes mass murders, then methods against domestic violence would do little to help the murdered Ukrainians. So, I changed my life completely. I joined the Army — because I had to."

Alina is from Kyiv. She's in her mid-thirties, with a tired yet strong voice. Her military call sign is Fox, something that her friends used to call her long before the war. I try to see a resemblance; maybe it's the hair. It's short and brown, with a slight shade of red. Or maybe, it's Alina's love for animals—while on the front-line, she helped rescue many pets.

The medic worked across many different sectors before becoming a servicewoman—and never considered joining the army.

Right before the current war, Alina was a manager in a charitable organization. A psychologist by training, Alina was also pursuing her Ph.D. while doing consultancies on addressing domestic violence. Prior to her human rights involvement, Alina had been a sex worker, so in her advocacy she focused on the rights of people with addictions and sex workers.

The woman expected that Russia may invade Ukraine in that fateful February of 2022, so she made some preparations. She took a one-day course on medical aid, and in the early days of the full-scale war, started organizing psychological support groups—all while hiding from the missiles in the Kyiv subway and trying to get into the Territorial Defense to protect her country.

"I went to the military commission to sign up, but I didn't even reach it." Alina remembered how in late February, she was trying to join the army. "At the entrance, there was a security guy. He told me: 'You can write your name in this book, but they do not take girls unless they are professional medics.' And I was not," she said.

Despite this and the lack of support from her own family, Alina persisted.

She had an acquaintance in a military unit, who introduced her to the head medic there.

"The doctor asked: 'Are you afraid of blood?' Alina recalled. "I said: 'No.' 'Okay, let's go sign you up for the Armed Forces.' So I did my application, and fifteen minutes later they gave me a gun."

In the Army

"I became the senior medic of the squadron right away," Alina said. "I started going to block posts in Kyiv even though I was not required to—just so I lived in the same rhythm as everyone else."

It looked like this: the volunteer stood three hours at a security checkpoint at the Victory Prospect, one of the most important parts of Kyiv. Then, they had six hours of rest, and then, the same routine again, all the time.

"I was going there with my gun," Alina added. "I had no bulletproof vest. I got winter pants and a light jacket only, but I was happy with the pants still. On top of the light jacket, I wore an additional one, and on top of that, I put on my military uniform, so it looked a bit more formal. This is how I went to the posts. There was shooting, and there were rockets and missiles nearby."

Alina started her work on March 5, 2022. She had no helmet, and her unit had no army food, but local restaurants cooked and brought food for them. It was difficult to provide anything logistically because there were heavy battles around Kyiv. Besides, there was not enough ammunition for everyone. Later, Ukraine started getting aid from different countries, and logistics improved with the Russians retreating, so the army got better equipped.

In the early days, there were also no real medical trainings. Alina's skills were limited at best back then, all she had was that one-day training from before the invasion plus her bachelor's degree in psychology.

However, there was a shortage of professional medics during these early days of the war, which meant a lot of self-education for Alina. She also asked advice from more experienced doctors as she studied on her own.

"I did not get any education on tactical medicine at first," she recalled. "Later, my teammates and I got good and accessible classes so we studied there. We kind of went illegally because the head medic of the entire unit was against this. H he said he'd train us himself but ended up doing nothing."

During the early days, her squadron did not have any wounded, but it also had no other medics. Alina had access to a limited amount of medicines and a large number of people with high blood pressure among the members of the Territorial Defense units in Kyiv she was serving. Back then, Covid was also going strong.

Later, Alina's skills improved greatly after months of practical work and real classes in tactical medicine. The system also improved over time. Now she has a platoon medical assistant with the right education, and there are experts from the medical unit who advise her as well as the battalion medic who can treat the patients.

Saving and Losing

"After Kyiv, I moved to Kyiv region, on the border with Belarus," Alina recalled. "There was always a big threat of invasion as troops on the other side were acting provocatively. They also used their drones, but they never invaded."

Afterward, the woman ended up in the east, in Donbas.

In her squadron, she quickly got to know the people and saw how soldiers with very different worldviews worked together.

"As a senior military medic of the squadron, I take care of all the wounded," Alina said. "Those with heavy wounds require a lot of attention. They are relocated from hospital to hospital, and they need a lot of stuff. I also take care of their papers because in the army, a person cannot go to a doctor without a rapport that's signed by the commander, and then the head medic needs to write a referral, which later needs to be registered in the squadron," she added.

Army bureaucracy is disheartening. Yet, it pales with the actual work of saving lives. The routine is that there is no routine but the days are always different. A medic is always waiting for something to happen, it's their responsibility to be on call, ready to treat the wounded after an attack. In between, the medics check their supplies, train soldiers on first aid, and wait again.

Alina explained that her squadron was lucky because the fighters were not wounded right away.

"Due to the specifics of this war, the main thing is to train the soldiers," the medic explained. "They are the ones next to wounded comrades, and our key task was to teach them how to behave around them. I am very proud of my fellow soldiers because they learned how to take care of themselves and how to aid others. This is crucial because they can be in a situation when they are hurt, and there is nobody around."

For Alina, there is a big difference between taking care of a stranger and taking care of one's comrade. Knowing a soldier makes it much harder to see their pain or death. While on the frontline, Alina has seen a lot of deaths of comrades who became dear to her.

"The worst part is seeing the loss of people I know," she said. "I know personally and am often friends with the soldiers who later get wounded. I have friends among the killed ones. I knew their wives. These were the people with whom we slept, ate, and lived together."

"A medic got killed," Alina sighed. "His name was Yura, call sign 'Tourist.' He was my close friend from the early days. He promised to come to my wedding. But he won't come there. I was friends with his wife. This is the worst."

"We Should Not Have Been Here"

Alina says that does not take care of herself psychologically while on the frontline. For her, it's a problem for later, something impossible to deal with while the fighting continues.

"You cannot do anything to feel good in these conditions," Alina reflected. "There are some coping mechanisms; they work and protect you, which is great. Maybe, if we finished implementing the army reforms before the big war, we would have a differently built military psychology, so we would have mechanisms. However, for now, there are no such mechanisms. Also, we have very heavy battles, a very difficult enemy, and hard conditions. This is normal to feel that way."

"There is nothing good about the war," the medic added. "It should not have happened, and we should have all been home. I would like other countries to support us as much as possible so their own citizens would not need to go to fight. I do not recommend this to anyone. I would not have met these great army people otherwise, but we should not have been here."

Alina admits that she never wanted to join the army. Most members of the army had full civilian lives and did not plan to become soldiers. They took arms because they saw no choice but to fight for Ukraine.

Alina wants to shed light on soldiers who, like her, are defending their homeland. She started a podcast that collects testimonies of her colleagues with the hope that these would inspire more people to join the army. The podcast addresses military-related issues such as sexism, diversity, or unity.

"Once, before a battle, I was talking to one of our soldiers and telling him that it would be good to record a podcast with him," she remembered. She added, "He said he'd do it later but then, he died, so that later never happened. That's why I don't have time to postpone these stories. I record them now. I am not sure how they are perceived, and I do not think about it much. I just think it is important to talk that our army consists of a big part of volunteers who used to work in IT, civil society, or media. They are all soldiers now because we are at war."

"I heard volunteers' stories all the time, and I realized it was necessary to record them now while these people are still alive, and before this topic became some marble tablet in a public school," the medic continued. "It is necessary to hear and know this now."

Alina believes that spreading the word can also help keep the war relevant for people outside of Ukraine so her home country could get more aid to stop the Russian aggression.

"Right now, we, with our blood, are stopping a huge menace for the entire Europe," she said. "And with our blood, we're also winning the world some time to unite, transform, and be ready to fight off this menace. I hope the world will use this time as effectively as possible. Otherwise, they are next. Russia would like the war to prolong this war, so it becomes forgotten."

UKRAINIAN VOICES

Collected by Andreas Umland

Book series "Ukrainian Voices"

Sergiy Korsunsky, Kobe Gakuin University, Japan
Nadiia Koval, Kyiv School of Economics, Ukraine
Volodymyr Kravchenko, University of Alberta, Edmonton
Oleksiy Kresin, NAS Koretskiy Institute of State and Law, Kyiv
Anatoliy Kruglashov, Fedkovych National University, Chernivtsi
Andrey Kurkov, PEN Ukraine, Kyiv
Ostap Kushnir, Lazarski University, Warsaw
Taras Kuzio, National University of Kyiv-Mohyla Academy
Serhii Kvit, National University of Kyiv-Mohyla Academy
Yuliya Ladygina, The Pennsylvania State University, USA
Yevhen Mahda, Institute of World Policy, Kyiv
Victoria Malko, California State University, Fresno, USA
Yulia Marushevska, Security and Defense Center (SAND), Kyiv
Myroslav Marynovych, Ukrainian Catholic University, Lviv
Oleksandra Matviichuk, Center for Civil Liberties, Kyiv
Mykhailo Minakov, Kennan Institute, Washington, USA
Anton Moiseienko, The Australian National University, Canberra
Alexander Motyl, Rutgers University-Newark, USA
Vlad Mykhnenko, University of Oxford, United Kingdom
Vitalii Ogiienko, Ukrainian Institute of National Remembrance, Kyiv
Olga Onuch, University of Manchester, United Kingdom
Olesya Ostrovska, Museum "Mystetskyi Arsenal," Kyiv
Anna Osypchuk, National University of Kyiv-Mohyla Academy
Oleksandr Pankieiev, University of Alberta, Edmonton
Oleksiy Panych, Publishing House "Dukh i Litera," Kyiv
Valerii Pekar, Kyiv-Mohyla Business School, Ukraine
Yohanan Petrovsky-Shtern, Northwestern University, Chicago
Serhii Plokhy, Harvard University, Cambridge, USA
Andrii Portnov, Viadrina University, Frankfurt-Oder, Germany
Maryna Rabinovych, Kyiv School of Economics, Ukraine
Valentyna Romanova, Institute of Developing Economies, Tokyo
Natalya Ryabinska, Collegium Civitas, Warsaw, Poland

Darya Tsymbalyk, University of Oxford, United Kingdom
Vsevolod Samokhvalov, University of Liege, Belgium
Orest Semotiuk, Franko National University, Lviv
Viktoriya Sereda, NAS Institute of Ethnology, Lviv
Anton Shekhovtsov, University of Vienna, Austria
Andriy Shevchenko, Media Center Ukraine, Kyiv
Oxana Shevel, Tufts University, Medford, USA
Pavlo Shopin, National Pedagogical Dragomanov University, Kyiv
Karina Shyrokykh, Stockholm University, Sweden
Nadja Simon, freelance interpreter, Cologne, Germany
Olena Snigova, NAS Institute for Economics and Forecasting, Kyiv
Ilona Solohub, Analytical Platform "VoxUkraine," Kyiv
Iryna Solonenko, LibMod - Center for Liberal Modernity, Berlin
Galyna Solovei, National University of Kyiv-Mohyla Academy
Sergiy Stelmakh, NAS Institute of World History, Kyiv
Olena Stiazhkina, NAS Institute of the History of Ukraine, Kyiv
Dmitri Stratievski, Osteuropa Zentrum (OEZB), Berlin
Dmytro Stus, National Taras Shevchenko Museum, Kyiv
Frank Sysyn, University of Toronto, Canada
Olha Tokariuk, Center for European Policy Analysis, Washington
Olena Tregub, Independent Anti-Corruption Commission, Kyiv
Hlib Vyshlinsky, Centre for Economic Strategy, Kyiv
Mychailo Wynnyckyj, National University of Kyiv-Mohyla Academy
Yelyzaveta Yasko, NGO "Yellow Blue Strategy," Kyiv
Serhy Yekelchyk, University of Victoria, Canada
Victor Yushchenko, President of Ukraine 2005-2010, Kyiv
Oleksandr Zaitsev, Ukrainian Catholic University, Lviv
Kateryna Zarembo, National University of Kyiv-Mohyla Academy
Yaroslav Zhalilo, National Institute for Strategic Studies, Kyiv
Sergei Zhuk, Ball State University at Muncie, USA
Alina Zubkovych, Nordic Ukraine Forum, Stockholm
Liudmyla Zubrytska, National University of Kyiv-Mohyla Academy